The Internet Case Study Book

Ed. Rob Ford/Julius Wiedemann

TASCHEN

"Success is the ability to go
from one failure to another
with no loss of enthusiasm."

Sir Winston Churchill ^(1874–1965)

Contents

Foreword

by <u>Julius Wiedemann</u>

Foreword

More digital and more humanised

Every bit as interesting as looking at all the technology that surrounds us, and which infiltrates our lives on a daily basis, is to think about how we learn with it all. Many of the gadgets, devices, programs, and websites that we use so often are so new that we usually do not stop to think about the deep effect they have on our lifestyle. Maybe this is because most of the time they offer a positive change, and so we simply take them for granted. In my opinion digital media does not decrease the value or cause other, older ways of doing things to vanish. On the contrary, it helps us realise how good all these things are, and how they have a different function, which might change over time, but remains there, somehow, transformed.

We have abundant examples in communication, from painting to photography, from live concerts to radio, from cinema to VCR. The typical readers of this book write probably monthly more emails than their parents wrote letters in an entire decade. But if you receive a handwritten letter today, it holds more value than it ever did. This fragmented world of communication channels can sometimes be magical.

"If you are afraid of committing mistakes, the chances of coming up with something new are minimal."

The two words that govern the world of communication today are relationship and interactivity. These are not new concepts. They have always existed. But the Internet created not just the perfect tool to bind them together, it has offered a new way of seeing how people relate to each other, and in the case of the examples in this book (with its profusion of commercial work), how brands relate to their public. The companies and people investing seriously in finding new breakthroughs may spend months or days in order to achieve great results. The size of budgets can be likewise very different, ranging from a couple of thousand to a couple of million. There is so much experimentation out there that it is sometimes too difficult to distinguish right or wrong, fast or slow, cheap or expensive, or even if there has been return on investment.

One thing is for sure, the companies and people working in this area are learning earlier, every day, and faster. If you are afraid of committing mistakes, the chance of you coming up with something new is minimal. And the cases presented in this book all come from professionals who do not fear new challenges. This makes this publication a very special one.

"It's been proven that old and new can still coexist, and can add value to each other."

Another special thing about this publication is the work that Rob Ford has been doing for almost a decade to improve the quality of design by sharing the best achievements online. When we teamed up to produce books, we firstly asked ourselves if those books would actually be as necessary as they proved to be. But we accepted the risk and worked hard to give readers real value, a record of something they could keep for a long time, and take everywhere, to show to friends, clients, and colleagues. We combined our experience and talked to the best people in their fields.

The shift to digital is not a question of "if", but "when and how". But once more, it's been proven that old and new can still coexist, and can add value to each other. We both look forward to the years ahead.

Julius Wiedemann

Introduction

by <u>Rob Ford</u>,
Favourite Website Awards (FWA)

Following on from the welcome reception of the last book, Guidelines for Online Success, Julius and I wanted to go deeper into some of the world's most impressive websites by exploring how these sites came about and featuring the proven results that made them stand out from the crowd.

What we have compiled here is a number of case studies, all of which follow a set formula so that the reader will feel in control throughout the book. Each case is broken down into four sections: "The Brief" explains the direction the client gave; "The Challenge" explains what the agency faced when creating the project; "The Solution" runs through the finished project, and "The Results" gives you an insight into how successful the project became.

> **"Julius and I wanted to go deeper into some of the world's most impressive websites by exploring how these sites came about."**

Each case study gives you some added information, including a link to the project, or a quote on it from either the client, a user, a member of the team who created it or, on occasion, myself. You'll also find credits for each example plus awards won, not forgetting some really eye-catching images.

One of the areas I was most looking forward to researching when putting this book together was the statistical information for each example. I am a total stats junkie and you can often find me looking through the daily stats for my websites. It's always a great buzz to see how many people are looking at a website, where they are from, how much time they are spending on a site, etc. So, it was great, and also very hard at times, to be able to receive some stats for each case study to show you how truly impressive each of the examples is and why they had deservedly gained their place in The Internet Case Study Book.

You'll find some statistical information in some of the "Results" sections but keep an eye out for the "HOT STATS" as this is where we are highlighting the impressive stats. As we move through the book the stats differ from one example to another so you'll always find an impressive number. I had to work really hard with the agencies in the book and their clients to get some of the stats released to us so I really hope you enjoy seeing them.

My favourite stat in the book has to be the following, from the Dominos.com case study: "113 quintillion pizza variation possibilities"!! Rest assured that the stats are not all as extreme as that as we have tried very hard to cover a wide range of projects, from small to large, so that you, the reader, can find something that is in line with your own business or client base.

"My favourite stat in the book has to be from the Dominos.com case study – 113 quintillion pizza variation possibilities!"

This book is divided into five chapters: Campaigns; E-Commerce; Promotional; Social Media; Corporate. Each chapter has been introduced by people at the pinnacle of this industry.

Chapter 1: Campaigns, is introduced by Jeff Goodby, founder and co-chairman of Goodby, Silverstein & Partners. Jeff sets the stage for a chapter that looks at world-leading and highly acclaimed campaigns, featuring example sites like the frightening Hotel 626, a campaign that allows the user to interact via the Web, mobile, and webcam, and whose website is only open from 6 p.m. to 6 a.m. (it's a scary experience and not for those afraid of the dark!).

Chapter 2: E-Commerce, is introduced by Alex Bogusky, chief creative officer at Crispin Porter + Bogusky. Alex opens up a chapter that spans a number of industries, including a case study on CP+B's own Dominos.com, as well as cases on brands like Adobe, Diesel, Volkswagen, and more. Some of the cases even reveal some financials, which were tough statistics to extract from the relevant clients but I am pleased they did as this is what's most important for any e-commerce website.

Chapter 3: Promotional, is introduced by Ajaz Ahmed, co-founder and chairman of AKQA. Ajaz leads us perfectly into this chapter with AKQA's own super-impressive Happy Christmas campaign which was an overnight phenomenon. With the likes of the Elf Yourself campaign, which received over 225 million visits, and other cases from industries covering food and drink, automotive, video games, entertainment and music, and... cage fighting, I'm sure you'll find this to be one of the most exciting chapters.

Chapter 4: Social Media, is introduced by Freddy Mini, CEO of Netvibes, the leading personalised startpage and widget marketing platform, serving more than 1,000 of the world's top agencies, brands, and publishers. Freddy starts by taking us through a very impressive Netvibes case study which incorporates over a thousand brands. This chapter touches on how the Web has changed in recent years as we have pretty much given control back to the people as we let the user decide what they want to see and even let them make the decisions about the sites they are on. It also includes studies on many community-style sites including the likes of the huge Last.fm, where I have one of my favourite quotes in the book from Last.fm's co-founder, Martin Stiksel: "music non stop."

"One of the areas I was most looking forward to when putting this book together was the statistical information for each example."

The final chapter in the book covers the world of Corporate sites and is introduced by Grégoire Assemat-Tessandier, global head of Digital – Bacardi Global Brands. We jump straight into this chapter with an impressive Bacardi.com case study and then move through some old and new sites, including the Site of The Year-winning Road Runner portal, which was the first big Flash-made portal to really set the world alight. We then look at websites from the likes of AT&T, Philips, EA, and others.

Finally, the book is perfectly rounded off by Lars Bastholm in the Afterword. Those of you who have a copy of *Guidelines for Online Success* will remember that Lars also wrote the last piece for that book as well and I couldn't think of anyone better to sign off this companion book either. Lars, who is now chief digital creative officer, Ogilvy North America, again perfectly summarises where we have been and where we could be going. If I can just finish up this book introduction with a few words from the wise man himself: "Let's keep in mind that the Internet as a brand-building medium is still only about 15 years old. It remains an unruly teenager trying to figure out its place in the world and what it all means." – Lars Bastholm, 2009.

I hope you enjoy this book and remember those famous words… do read this book, don't let it collect dust!

Rob Ford
Favourite Website Awards

Do
Read this book

Don't
Let it collect dust

Bio.
Rob Ford
Favourite Website Awards

Rob Ford, born England 1969, founded Favourite Website Awards (FWA) in May 2000, a recognition program for cutting-edge web design which has since received over 50 million site visits.

His work has been featured in numerous publications including *The Chicago Tribune*, *The Guardian*, *Penthouse*, and many Web-related magazines. He has judged for most of the industry award shows, contributes regularly to other well-known web design sites and magazines (from all corners of the globe), and writes a regular column in Adobe's *Edge* Newsletter.
–
www.robford.com
www.thefwa.com

Campaigns

Introduction by
Jeff Goodby, Goodby, Silverstein & Partners

01

We think it's a revolution. But there are still wide sectors of resistance, parts of the collective consciousness that lag unknowingly behind.

Give yourself this simple test:
If you still think that webfilms (yes, even viral ones) are part of the Internet's leading edge, please take one step backwards.

If you think that spending vast amounts of time on Facebook, Twitter, or, God knows, YouTube, proves your Internet literacy, take ten laps around the Wikidome.

If you've never been concerned about whether your Flash-based site works on an iPhone, here's a complete 2001 set of Wired magazine you'll find interesting.

Do you remember and feel condescendingly nostalgic at the mere mention of Webvan, eToys, Subservient Chicken, and Napster? This would be a good thing, I think.

The point is, people are beginning to be differentiated by their levels of sophistication when it comes to the Internet experience. We are making nuanced distinctions and judgments we didn't make in the early stages of this revolution (when our first takes were largely binary – things were either spectacular or boring). We are getting tired of things other people are not tired of yet. We are weary of certain common tricks.

"We are getting tired of things other people are not tired of yet. We are weary of certain common tricks."

This is a book that is aware of all this and has amassed the tools that will help us move into the next chapter. After seeing the work collected here, we will, I think, all realize even higher levels of Internet sophistication. We'll be pickier and more critical.

Marshall McLuhan said, "We drive into the future using only our rearview mirror." What you'll see here are the most recently passed parts of the road.

I have stopped calling these things websites and begun referring to them as "Internet experiences". Indeed, they suggest the early days of the novel, what it must have felt like in the 18th Century to read Fielding or Sterne. It was a time of big change. Stories that were previously straightforward and linear, handed down around campfires for generations, were suddenly replaced by highly personal accounts, operating on many levels. Simple myths became complex experience, suddenly examined from hundreds of different points of view. We are in the earliest phases of this transformation on the Internet. The Joyces and Tolstoys are still in the wings.

The best work you'll find in here foreshadows the truly exciting stuff that will happen to this medium in five or ten years. Instead of merely offering flashy graphics or a surface challenge like a shooting game, these are experiences that draw you in and take you down several levels. They involve you emotionally. You care about characters. You can viscerally *feel* a trip through a certain environment.

One of my favorites here is The Lost Ring, a perfect example of what I'm talking about. The "missing story" of Ariadne and a past Olympic drama is not only captivating and complex, it makes you feel the emotions of the heroine. It also resonantly evokes a past era with terrific graphics and historical detail.

"Clearly, we are seeing the beginnings of a new kind of Internet here. A new world in which corporations are forced to abandon the repetitive, insulting messages they've relied upon for so long."

Hotel 626 was launched around Halloween to celebrate Frito-Lay's "Flavor Graveyard", a program in which Doritos temporarily brings back certain flavors that have been phased out over the years. The experience is set in an abandoned insane asylum in Sweden, and you can only enter the site between 6.00 p.m. and 6.00 a.m., ensuring that your home is as dark and spooky as possible. Unusual details include startling, urgent instructions that are sent to your cell phone in real time, and a surreptitious snapshot of you that appears in a gallery of victims later in the story. The effect is truly scary.

There are things here that are simply undeniable fun, like Send-a-Sandcastle and Get the Glass. (The latter is so deep, it often takes players days to explore it.) HBO Voyeur exploits a basic human desire to watch in on others in the midst of their lives – an insight that led to an experience that won just about every big prize last year.

But some of the biggest leaps forward here are to be found in the arena of spectacular graphics. FarCry 2, Call of Duty, and Yoobot are all mesmerizing, beyond what could have been done even just one or two years ago. They are a tribute to the unheard-of speed with which things are changing, and the staggering number of late-night pizzas the world's true innovators are presently eating. I defy you to open these experiences without spending significant time in them.

Clearly, we are seeing the beginnings of a new kind of Internet here. It's something I've been predicting for quite a while, a new world in which corporations are forced to abandon the repetitive, insulting messages they've relied upon for so long. Instead, we will be seeing the corporate communicators scurry in the direction of what can only be called, well, entertainment.

"It's my belief that the world's successful companies will have significant entertainment arms, all of them, that will take over the role networks used to play on TV."

It's my belief that the world's successful companies will have significant entertainment arms, all of them, that will take over the role networks used to play on TV. Not just website experiences, but even movies and serial drama and comedies will be developed and funded by certain companies, and we'll go to their website to find these things. We'll hear: What's on Sony tonight? Nike is featuring a biopic about John McEnroe. Hey, they're playing the complete collection of old "Sopranos" on Cadillac.

But it is Internet experiences like the ones you'll find in here that are leading the way to the brave new world. This is already taking place, and I for one am on the bus.

In 1983, we began working for a startup called "Amazin' Software." We renamed it Electronic Arts and ran a press ad that brazenly asked, "Can a computer make you cry?" It seemed far-fetched in its day, shocking even. But damn if it hasn't happened to me, more than once even, in the midst of the world you'll find in these pages. Welcome to the new Internet of real emotion.

Jeff Goodby
Goodby, Silverstein & Partners

Bio.
<u>Jeff Goodby</u>
Goodby, Silverstein
& Partners

Jeff Goodby is founder and co-chairman of Goodby, Silverstein & Partners in San Francisco, the agency that is widely acclaimed for most successfully integrating traditional and digital media arts.

GS&P has been Agency of the Year in *Advertising Age*, *Adweek*, and *Creativity* magazines several times each, but has also been selected as Digital Agency of the Year in *Advertising Age*, *Business 2.0*, and by the One Club of New York.

Many of their campaigns – got milk?, the Budweiser Lizards, Hewlett-Packard "Invent", the National Basketball Association's "I Love This Game", and the E*TRADE chimpanzee among them – are in the permanent collection of the Museum of Modern Art in New York.

Goodby is also a director, printmaker, and illustrator whose work has appeared in *Time* and *Mother Jones*. In 2006 he was inducted into the Advertising Hall of Fame.
–
www.goodbysilverstein.com

"Welcome to the new Internet of real emotion."

Hotel 626

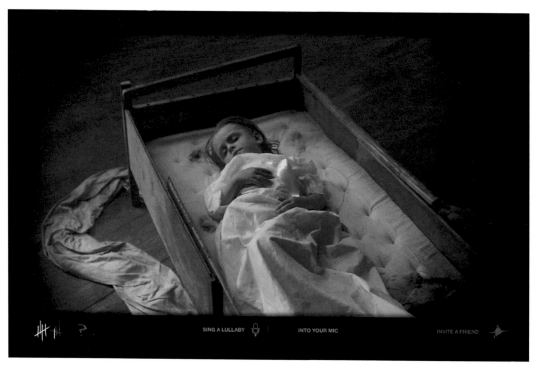

"Play at your own risk."
digg.com

The Brief
In the fall of 2008, Doritos brought back two of their most intense and popular flavors from the past. The two flavors – Taco and Four Cheese – were only on-shelf for a limited time and it was up to us to make people crave the old flavors they missed. In order to trigger flavor memories, we needed to create an experience so intense that our core target – a restless audience always in search of the most edgy content – would share it with friends.

The Challenge
We were tasked with honoring the resurrected flavors with a budget of less than $500,000 for both production and media. In order to reach our target, we realized that our limitations were actually a strength – investing millions of dollars on traditional media would fail to break through to this group in a credible and motivating way.

Instead, we decided to create incredibly intense, interactive content, and use our audience to spread the word. By blurring the lines between medium, message, and audience, we planned to launch these flavors in a completely unexpected, yet effective way.

Client
Frito-Lay

Credits
Goodby, Silverstein & Partners
www.goodbysilverstein.com
B-Reel
www.b-reel.com

Awards
FWA, New York Festivals, Andy,
One Show, Webby

www.hotel626.com

The Solution

Since the two flavors were essentially brought back from the dead, what if something dark came back with them? We decided to create a website with one goal – to scare the crap out of teenagers. You're living a nightmare in a live action, CG world never before seen in a website.

You're trapped in a haunted house and have to do whatever it takes to get out, like taking a picture of a psychopathic maid, singing a demon baby to sleep, and making it out of a madman's cell. This scare is personal. Hotel 626 uses your webcam to sneak a picture of you and shows it to you later in a serial killer's lair.

Your only salvation is a phone call on your actual cell phone that gives you directions on how to get out and knows your every move. To make it scarier, you have to play in the dark. Hotel 626 is only open from 6 p.m. to 6 a.m.

4 Million unique users

188 Countries visiting

13:34 Minutes average "stay" time

1.9 Million registrations

254 YouTube clips generated

The Results

Hotel 626 proved that you don't need to "advertise" quality digital content as long as the content is intense and engaging enough that it becomes viral. It lured over 4 million visitors down its dark hallway for an average "stay" of over 13 minutes, nearly four times the industry average.

Consumers were able to tweet their journeys so their friends found out they were "trapped in a room with a madman" or "running for their lives." Consumers also recorded videos of themselves playing and posted them on YouTube.

Hotel 626 was one of Contagious magazine's "Most Contagious" pieces of 2008 and FWA's People's Choice Award in 2008. It was also Adcritic's Most Viewed Interactive Item of 2008. The two resurrected flavors sold out in just three weeks.

BHF's Yoobot

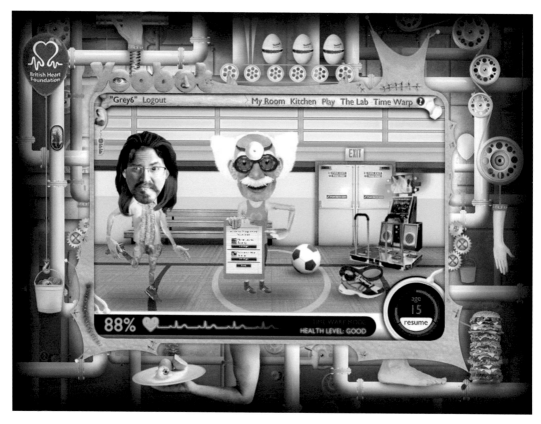

"Graphically, the site is fresh and youthful, and the quirky attention to detail is nice. On the whole it is fun, impactful, and smart."
NMA

The Brief
A third of the children in the UK are currently overweight. Childhood obesity is not just an issue of puppy fat; obese children are much more likely to become obese adults and suffer a premature death from cardiovascular disease. This problem is well documented through the media. We were tasked to get 11-13-year-old children to take greater responsibility for their own health. It is at this pivotal age that children start gaining more freedom in their choice of food and where future food habits are formed which last right through adulthood.

The Challenge
We needed to provide children with the basic tools to make good food choices. However, our target did not see the relevancy of addressing a threat to their long-term health. They have been targeted by messages in this area before and generally know what is good and bad food, but they feel "invincible" and they tend just to eat what they want. We needed to show them the future relevance of the problem on their terms, i.e. with impact and play value.

Client
British Heart Foundation

Credits
GREY London
www.grey.co.uk
BLOC Media
www.blocmedia.com
PHD Media
www.phd.co.uk

Awards
NMA

www.yoobot.co.uk

The Solution

An online game called Yoobot. Users register to create a free Yoobot – a customisable mini version of their self. Children can then experiment on their Yoobot by setting its diet and activity routines and watch the effect this diet would have on their health in the long run – physically and emotionally.

In order to succeed against millions of other sites, Yoobot needed that "must have" factor. This was created in schools with the help of a gaming-styled DVD, which was placed on a million school desks and six sheet posters around school catchment areas. It was also created through digital advertising, seeding to gaming sites and with the help of TVCs on Nickelodeon.

The Results

Since launching at the end of November 2008, Yoobot has had 1.06 million registrations with the average user interacting with the game for 18 minutes! Yoobot has also attracted high-profile media attention across the Internet, TV, and national and local newspapers. This included prominent features on the ITV news, the BBC, and GMTV, and was the third-fastest rising Internet search in the UK at launch (a more popular search term than Britney Spears). Children enjoyed playing Yoobot, with over 75% saying they enjoyed playing the game and that it was well worth their time.

Most importantly though, 78% of users said that they had improved their diets after playing the game and 57% said they had started taking more exercise. This claimed behaviour has even been backed up with food diaries showing that children were making the biggest changes in their snacking habits.

3 Million site
visits

1.15 Million Yoobots
created

18 Minutes average
time on site

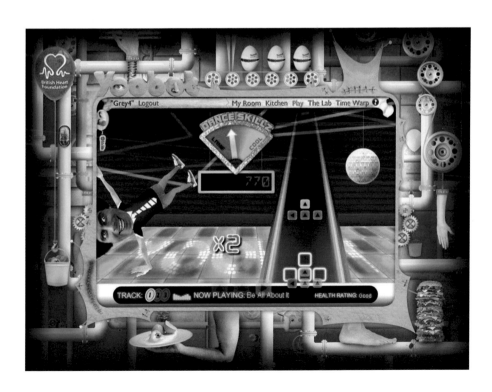

FarCry 2 Experience

"One of the best things about this site is that you almost feel like you are playing the real game."
Rob Ford, FWA

The Brief

Ubisoft wanted to develop a promotional experience site, part of a global marketing strategy, to support the release of their Far Cry 2 video game. As the game was proposing an Open World experience where the player could roam in 50km² of African landscape, the development team didn't want to release a demo of the game that would have given a false image of the game experience. Therefore, the Ubisoft online team proposed to translate all key features of the game into an interactive full-immersive website dedicated to 18-35-year-old video-game players that would be as accessible as possible. The main communication objectives were high-quality graphics and liberty of choice.

The Challenge

Translating high-quality graphics in a dynamic and user-friendly online experience was our main challenge. Creating a full experience using the graphics of the game itself was complex as the development of the title was still in progress. Consequently, we managed to create completely independent maps from those in the original game, more adapted to a short online experience, thanks to a powerful and flexible map editor engine. To illustrate the total freedom of choice in the game, a dedicated scenario was worked out beforehand. This helped us speed up and reduce as much as possible the recording of the game footage which is usually a resource- and time-consuming process.

Client
Ubisoft EMEA

Credits
group94
www.group94.com

Awards
FWA, Adobe Edge

www.farcrygame.com

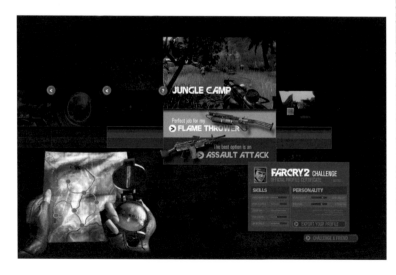

The Solution
Basically it is an interactive video story inviting the visitor for a "test assignment" to see if they are good enough for the real game. Hence we wrote a scenario for this assignment which was filmed with real game footage, presenting the visitor with different solutions to game situations. These choices influence the storyline and define the visitor's profile and skills. Biggest technical challenge was to create an engaging video experience by avoiding any loading sequence. Exactly as is the case in the real game…

The Results
Regarding our consumers, our goal was to push forward the gameplay visibility via this full-immersive website. As such we could not have been happier once we received some great feedback from our community telling us that they appreciated discovering the game through this online experience. The website attracted over 1.6 million visitors around the game release, and a time spent of over five minutes on average out of a total possible of eight minutes experience.

1.6 Million unique users
(first month)

5 Minutes average
time on site

21 Million Google
results

590,000 Registrations

The Alfa Romeo 159 Experience

"This is one of the most impressive
websites, on many levels, that we
have seen for some time."
Rob Ford, FWA

Client
Alfa Romeo France

Credits
Soleil Noir
www.soleilnoir.net

Awards
FWA, Adobe Max,
Club des Directeurs Artistiques

www.experience159.com

The Brief

Alfa Romeo France wanted to develop a website confirming Italian design and the embedded technology of the Alfa 159.

The major points of the brief were standing out in an interactive competition dominated by the US and Germany, and betting on an emotional approach which would confirm the strong and valuable relations to "Italianity", as too the notion of "discovery" and the possibility to subscribe for a test drive.

The Challenge

Incorporating the themes of security, sportiness, and design into a graphic universe clearly related to the brand proved to be a tough job.

Captivating the user's attention in order to allow them to discover different aspects of the vehicle meant creating a series of immersive, and graphically, rhythmically, and musically different categories.

It is this very diversity that serves the different aspects of the Alfa 159 so well. Moreover, it was exciting to define the technical challenge here, which seemed almost impossible, and working out how to offer this kind of interactive experience to a mass audience required several weeks of optimisations.

The Solution

We gambled on a site offering full-screen videos which gave maximum power to this realisation.

The colours of the brand logo used in each category, the alluring atmosphere of the home page, and the range of musical effects associated with the dynamics of the movements all helped immerse the user in a multimedia emotional experience.

The 3-D modelling of the car and the important work on the scenes permitted us to go even further in building its universe and contributed to the wow effect of the site.

The Results

This different approach to a format for communication within the car market created a strong interest. Even more interesting was the worldwide diffusion of a website which was 100% French. However, even if France remains the top country in terms of site visitors, it is worth noting that since the website was successfully diffused all round the world this is a reassurance that the idea that the transmission of the emotion we wanted to share wasn't hindered by linguistic barriers.

1 Million visits

1,000 Qualified test drives

123 Cars sold via the website

100 Countries visiting

UNIQLOCK

"A completely UNIQ experience!
Intriguing, original and addictive to
watch, this pioneering experience
has taken the web by storm."
Rob Ford, FWA

The Brief
UNIQLO was seeking an innovative way to build its brand awareness internationally, and promote its business expansion into the global market. We recognised the 70 million blogs worldwide as a powerful buzz-building medium, and created a functional and entertaining blog widget for the bloggers to spread the brand globally.

The Challenge
The campaign concept we needed to develop was the fusion of a clock which functions as a blog utility, time signalling music, and dance performance videos, with UNIQLO clothing. We named it UNIQLOCK.
    As a 100% UNIQLO branded widget, this automatically became a tool to connect UNIQLO and the world's bloggers.

Client
UNIQLO

Credits
Projector inc.
www.projector.jp

Awards
FWA, Cannes, One Show,
Clio, New York Festival, D&AD,
NY ADC, TIAA

www.uniqlock.jp

The Solution

As a teaser, we uploaded 16 audition videos on to YouTube. Then we launched the UNIQLOCK site to start distributing the blog widget. The numerous dance videos and the clock counter appearing seamlessly one after another makes viewers eager to see more.

Since the widget plays all year round, 24/7, the dancers change their outfits according to the season. The bloggers were motivated by seeing the website's world map which visualised the expansion of all the users. Screensavers and shop installations were also released to enhance the UNIQLOCK experience, from personal desktops to the UNIQLO stores.

The Results

This campaign captured worldwide recognition on the largest scale in the history of the Internet, thereby achieving its mission of raising brand recognition of UNIQLO to a world-class level. It earned top honours at FWA, One Show Interactive (Best Of Show), the CLIO Awards (Interactive Grand Prix), Cannes Lions (Titanium Grand Prix, Cyber Grand Prix), D&AD (Black Pencil, Yellow Pencil), and NY ADC(Hybrid Cube). With over 276 million site visits to date this has become a global phenomenon.

276 Million site visits

67,642 Widgets created

93 Countries visiting

1 Million YouTube views

175,000 Screensaver downloads

The Eco Zoo

Mrs. Roo

Family : marsupial. Genus : kangaroo.

Born with her own bag. She cannot walk backwards. Apparently, she is a positive thinking animal who just keeps on going forward.

× Pop-Up Book ⸱→

©ENJIN Inc. ©McCANN ERICKSON Japan, Inc.

Japanese

"Exemplary execution in development, animation and design truly makes this site a one of a kind experience that deserves the full bag of gold."
Jens Karlsson, Your Majesty, USA

back

She is a kangaroo who likes to think things through.

©ENJIN Inc. ©McCANN ERICKSON Japan, Inc.

The Brief

"The Eco Zoo" is a picture book-style educational website created by McCann Frickson Japan and Enjin. The Zoo started out as a picture book that told the stories of various eco-friendly animals that had natural assets that helped them be "green", like a kangaroo with a "recycle pocket", for example. The intention was to inspire both children and adults alike to think about the environment and how they can become more environmentally conscious. The website expands on the picture book idea and creates a 3-D world using Flash technology. The experience is like flipping through a virtual pop-up book. Our hope was that this device would entertain young visitors from all over the world, while at the same time teaching them the importance of environmental conservation.

The Challenge

Our challenge was to take a complex theme like the environment, which contains elements that may be hard to understand or seem contradictory, and present it in a way that even children can understand and enjoy. Also, since all of this started out as a picture book, we wanted to continue with the analogue feel in the website's execution and navigation. ROXIK's Kido-san's incredible skill in technique and expression enabled us to achieve this at a very high level.

Client
Creative Initiative

Credits
Enjin Inc.
www.en-jin.jp
McCann Erickson Japan Inc.
www.mccann.co.jp
ROXIK
www.roxik.com
Aoyama Creative Studio
http://acsmov.com

Awards
FWA, MOBIUS, Asia Interactive,
Adobe Edge, Yahoo!, NY ADC,
ADFEST, NY Festival,
Tokyo Interactive

www.ecodazoo.com

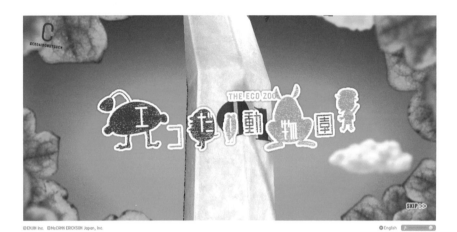

©ENJIN Inc. ©McCANN ERICKSON Japan, Inc.

©ENJIN Inc. ©McCANN ERICKSON Japan, Inc.

The Solution

To make environmental protection a concern for all people by means of the website.

The ultimate goal is to sustain our current earthly environment, so it's important to sustain this site as well.

The whole issue of the environment may never have arisen if human beings did not exist. That's how we came to choose animals as the point of view through which we wanted to look at this problem. Animals living in the natural world are innately eco-friendly in their lifestyles, and as soon as we realised that we couldn't choose any other perspective.

The Results

This site was not launched for commercial reasons, so we do not have any effectiveness measurements other than awards and articles. The site won the FWA Site of the Year, an international competition which had over 14 million visits, 12 finalists, 80 international judges, two rounds of voting and just one winner... The Eco Zoo.

We just hope that we'll see its influence on the next generation.

660,000
Unique users

950,000
Page views

12
International awards won

HBO Voyeur

"An excellent mix of technology and
theme that's completely engrossing
with many slices and saccades."
Jon McVey, Communication Arts
Interactive Annual 14 Juror

The Brief

For the last decade, HBO has unequivocally been the best storyteller, but in recent years broadcast and cable networks have upped the ante – producing programming with higher production values and more complex characters/storylines than seen in the past. As a result, our campaign goal was to fortify HBO against increasing competition by strengthening the brand's relationship with "super-fans".

Incredibly engaged in all forms of media, super-fans seek intelligent, cutting-edge entertainment experiences. They pride themselves in seeking out the best in entertainment, not only to explore different perspectives, but also to look smart and interesting to others. Super-fans recognize HBO as one of the few brands that respects their intelligence. They don't just watch HBO programs – they're completely involved and engaged before, during and after a show.

The Challenge

We know super-fans are passionate about HBO programming, but our task was to ignite this same level of passion around the HBO brand, by reinforcing its essence as the leading, most innovative storyteller.

We wanted a piece of communication that said: HBO is the greatest storyteller in the world and they tell those stories not just in TV, but in a wide variety of media. Instead of creating a campaign that just said those things, we created a campaign that demonstrated those things.

HBO Voyeur took the act of watching, already an integral part of the HBO brand experience, and intensified it. Viewers became essential players within the story – their gaze the very essence of the concept: sometimes the best stories are the ones we weren't meant to see.

Client
HBO

Credits
BBDO New York
www.bbdo.com
Big Spaceship
www.bigspaceship.com

Awards
Addys, Adobe, Andy's, ADC, AICP, Cannes, Clios, Communication Arts, CTAM Mark, D&AD, Design Week, FWA, Global Media Awards, HOW, London International, New York Festivals, Obie, One Show, Promax, Webby

http://qa.hbo.com/hbovoyeur
Username: voyeur
Password: 3agleey3

The Solution

In order to encourage the participation beyond passive viewing that is critical to super-fans' experience with the brand, HBO Voyeur was expressed as a multi-media, multi-platform program, each touch-point acting as an invitation to engage with the project as a whole.

HBOvoyeur.com was the online hub of this multi-platform storytelling experience. At center stage was a film made up of interconnected stories within eight apartments of a random urban dwelling. Each apartment was a single-take performance to heighten the effect of window-peeping.

If users chose to explore deeper into the cityscape beyond, they found four new stories featuring other city dwellers. In total, there was over two hours of filmed content, a behind-the-story blog (thestorygetsdeeper.com), six custom soundtracks, and downloadable extras including screensavers and video for PCs and mobile devices.

The Results

Over 1 million users visited HBOvoyeur.com within the first three weeks (Google Analytics). The campaign and site were mentioned in over 500 blogs, prompting conversations and debate (Nielsen BuzzMetrics). An ancillary site, thestorygetsdeeper.com, generated over 1 million page views in the first six weeks (WebStatistics).

HBO Voyeur had a strong and positive effect on super-fans' perception of the HBO brand – a hard task when they already had such strong positive feelings to begin with.

- 74% said Voyeur set the HBO brand apart
- 72% claimed it made them think HBO is better than other networks
- 60% said it made them more interested in the HBO brand

1 Million site visits (first 3 weeks)

9 Minutes average time on site

1.6 Million unique users

10,000 Downloads

500 Blog mentions

Digital Concert Hall

"Though I very much enjoy living on a gorgeous little island with 150 inhabitants on the Polar Circle, it is somehow not quite the place to be when it comes to watching classical music live. The Digital Concert Hall gives me the chance to watch my favourite orchestra any time I want – and in a way, it's better than live. I'd never be able to see Sir Simon's conducting with the same detail in the real concert hall – the quality is just exceptional."
Michael Rintellen, Rødøy

The Brief

With most concerts and tours sold out in advance, the Berliner Philharmoniker would like to share their music with a broader audience. To offer the experience of witnessing their concerts live whilst creating an ever-growing archive of recordings is very dear to them.

Create a website that conveys the live concert experience, more beautiful than YouTube but less playful and distracting than Second Life. The platform must be easy enough to use for all ages and all cultures and must adhere to the highest standards in audio and video quality.

The Challenge

Having produced the first classical music LP, the first classical music CD, and starring in several big-screen documentaries, the Berliner Philharmoniker has a strong tradition of embracing new media and, as one of the world's best orchestras, sets very high demands when it comes to creative collaboration and technical fidelity.

The opportunity: unprecedented. Experience live music on the Internet? Done. Live classical music? Ok, you can find it if you look. But live concert streaming, for a global audience, with CD-quality sound, in HighDef video, on a digital platform dedicated to arguably the world's best orchestra? Never been done before.

Of course, as pioneers in both analogue and digital recording, the Berliner Philharmoniker has a long history of firsts – our challenge, then, was to add to this list by building the first DCH (digital concert hall).

Client
Berlin Phil Media GmbH

Credits
argonauten G2, Berlin
www.argonauteng2.de

Awards
FWA, ADC, LeadAwards, One Show

http://dch.berliner-philharmoniker.de

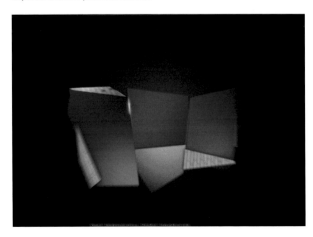

325,000 — Site visits

4 — Million page views

15,000 — Registered users

149 — Countries visiting

The Solution

A fully interactive Adobe Flash-based website on top of a complex software platform for managing content, payments, and user accounts. Design and interface reinterpret Hans Scharoun's once revolutionary architecture of the Berliner Philharmonie, creating a sense of depth and anticipation as one navigates towards the inside of the concert hall where the music awaits.

The Digital Concert Hall is highly scalable for sudden peaks in visitors during live concerts, and guarantees fast download speeds from all corners of the planet thanks to a special content delivery network. The transmissions are in HD video and superb AAC audio, encoded in the same format as used in Blu-Ray discs.

The Results

The first concert alone attracted 2,500 paying viewers, more than the capacity of the Berliner Philharmonie. A worldwide and unanimously enthusiastic press coverage, extensive blogging, several design awards, and a huge influx of subscribers to the orchestra's Facebook and YouTube communities followed suit. More than 1,000 season passes were sold within the first weeks.

Call of Duty

"Faced with complex requirements and impossible delivery timeline, 2Advanced delivered a global portal that met these criteria and in time for the reveal of Call of Duty: World at War. The site has generated over 1 MM+ registered users by the time we shipped the game, four months after the initial launch. The success of the Call of Duty Headquarters speaks for itself and we're thrilled with its continued growth."
Carlson Choi, Head of Digital,
Activision Blizzard

Client
Activision Blizzard

Credits
2Advanced Studios
www.2advanced.com

Awards
Finalist "2009 Most Clickable Gaming
Site" – 2009 MI6 Gaming Conference

www.callofduty.com

The Brief
Since 2003, the award-winning Call of Duty video game franchise has topped sales charts and user reviews for its intense single-player game play and addictive multi-player modes. There are five major instalments in the Call of Duty series, plus multiple expansion packs, and the game series has been set in World War II as well as modern warfare times. For the first time in the franchise's history, the Call of Duty Headquarters was set to house all fans across the various titles under a single online destination. The new COD HQ needed to accommodate the new, younger generation of gamers coming to the series for the first time, while also catering to the older players who have followed the franchise over the years.

The Challenge
Since the games are set in different eras, the challenge was to create an online home suitable for all titles as well as for multiple types of players across a range of demographics. In addition, this online destination needed to truly stand out amongst the highly intense, incredibly competitive video game space. The site needed a strong visual aesthetic, and simplistic user interface, while also delivering a complex set of cutting-edge features and interactive components. Considering the huge success of the Call of Duty franchise, the site needed optimum performance under extremely heavy traffic levels, while delivering large packets of data on a minute by minute basis. Lastly, the site needed to support five languages while addressing various location-specific requirements for content delivery.

The Solution

The COD HQ houses the traditional information expected of a gaming website: product information, game assets, up-to-date news and RSS feeds, as well as active forums for gamers to interact with one another. There is a competitive community ranking system, which mirrors the in-game ranking system, to reward members with badges for participation in the site's polls, trivia questions, competitions, and even in-game achievements. Members can customize their site avatar with these badge rewards to tout their prominence both in the game and on the website. The site goes even further to deliver real-time syndication of in-game statistics. Players can join multi-player matches from their Xbox 360/PS3/NDS, compete against opponents online, and then visit the site to compare their results against other players'. Entire player histories can be accessed so members can examine their performance and measure their improvements over time. Users even have access to timeline-based heat maps of recent battles to see where team members are succeeding or failing to improve their strategies better.

1.6 — Million registered members

250 — Million page views

20 — Million unique users

1.3 — Million forum threads

52 — Million Google results

The Results

The success of the COD HQ was instant and continues to flourish. Call of Duty fans immediately flooded registrations to access the all-new features. In the first week of launch alone, the site received 1 million visits and 5 million page views. Currently, there are 1.6 million+ registered and active members. The forums have 1.3 million+ posts. The site has received over 250 million page views since launching in June 2008. In terms of gaming statistics, over 400K players have linked their accounts to their in-game Xbox Live and/or Playstation Network accounts. Over 1,000 data points are saved per player, while hundreds of data points are saved for every multi-player match played. This extraordinary amount of data is served up across a complex server farm and enterprise level content delivery network. The site successfully merges all Call of Duty fans under a single URL and offers gamers an online experience that is truly tied to their in-game experience. Players can now stay immersed in the Call of Duty universe while away from their gaming consoles.

The Lost Ring

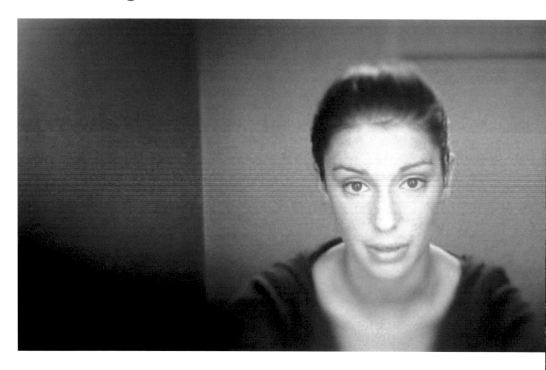

The Brief

McDonald's has been a long-time official sponsor of the Olympic Games and saw the 2008 Olympics in Beijing as a great opportunity to leverage the spirit and scale of the Olympics to increase brand relevance among young adults worldwide (defined as 18–34). McDonald's tasked AKQA with reinvigorating young adults' brand affinity with McDonald's globally.

The Challenge

As AKQA brainstormed concepts, the agency looked to strategically leverage the confluence of three global forces: 1. McDonald's, the world's biggest local food restaurant, 2. the emerging connectedness of global youth culture, driven by the digital revolution, and 3. the communal spirit of the Olympic Games, more than just a competition, an international culture of coming-together.

Most importantly there was the acknowledgement to respect young adults' sensitivity and a tendency to tune out traditional marketing messages. So they developed a program that delivered a truly authentic, uncompromised, and engaging experience.

This led us to AKQA's guiding strategic insight: rather than focus on connecting young adults to the McDonald's brand, focus on how McDonald's can connect young adults around the world to each other.

"This was the year of innovation for McDonald's, and The Lost Ring was the centerpiece of that and an event that allowed us to engage young people like never before."
Mary Dillon, Global Chief Marketing Officer, McDonald's

Client
McDonald's

Credits
AKQA
www.akqa.com

Awards
Promotion Marketing Awards
(Reggie), Adweek Buzz Awards,
AICP Show, OMMA, One Show

www.thelostring.com

The Solution

AKQA created a global alternate-reality game entitled "The Lost Ring" inviting players from across the world to join forces online and in the real world, as they investigate forgotten mysteries and urban legends of the ancient games. The Lost Ring recognizes McDonald's historic sponsorship of the Olympic Games, and brings the spirit of the Games to people around the world.

To date, The Lost Ring has been the world's biggest and first truly global alternate-reality game. It encouraged players from over 100 countries to reach across geographic, cultural, and linguistic borders to unite in solving the mystery of six amnesiac Olympians who competed in an ancient, lost Olympic sport: Labyrinth Running.

What made the ARG even more unique was that it launched completely unbranded. The game made its debut via seeding of packages containing cryptic, mysterious information to prominent bloggers and ARG-players around the world. Instantly, buzz began spreading: players began to blog, post package content, communicate via user-generated message boards and wikis, and the game was on.

From March through the culmination of the Olympic Games in August The Lost Ring evolved into a cultural phenomenon. Players pasted together clues from websites, videos, and blogs, as well as from physical artefacts hidden in dozens of historical sites around the world. Players met up in the real world to practice Labyrinth Running and ultimately hunt down five bronze rings across five continents engraved with the final clues of the game. As the game approached its conclusion, Olympic champion Edwin Moses joined the players in their quest to solve the global mystery.

The game's finale ultimately occurred in Beijing aligned with the Olympic closing ceremonies. It brought together the game's main protagonists who competed with multiple-player teams around the world in a time-aligned "Multiverse Olympiad" of Labyrinth Running.

The Results

4.8 million views and site visits globally; over 2.9 million people in over 110 countries participated in the game, 28% from North America (source: WebTrends Analytics & Agency Tracking). Among people aware of the game, 73% agreed that "It brought people together globally".

Brand favorability ratings among participants increased by 6.1%. Respondents agreeing with "I have positive things to say about the brand" increased by 5.3%. Respondents agreeing with "Is a brand I speak more favorably about than others" increased by 6.2%.

The ARG coined a new marketing term, "dark marketing", as defined by Wired magazine: **Dark marketing** *n.* Discreetly sponsored online and real-world entertainment intended to reach hipster audiences that would ordinarily shun corporate shilling. McDonald's is the latest mega-brand to adopt this paradoxical promotional tool, with an alternate-reality game called The Lost Ring, nearly devoid of golden arches.

4.8 Million site visits

2.9 Million unique users

110 Participating countries

6.1 Percent brand ratings increase

Hilton Journeys

"A seductive website that uses
delightful animations to guide
the user through the experience."
Rob Ford, FWA

Client
Hilton

Credits
BLITZ Agency
www.blitzagency.com

Awards
W3 Awards

http://www.blitzagency.com/
ourWork.aspx?brandId=&project=80
&template=cs

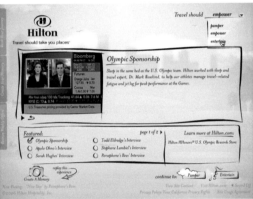

The Brief

As Hilton revitalized their brand, they wanted to impress upon business travelers, as well as recruiting a younger audience, that their hotel stay was much more than that. It was no longer about simply getting from point A to point B, it was a journey, an enjoyable experience that is meant to enhance the trip. Using an integrated approach, Hilton sought out BLITZ to create an online destination that built upon the offline message, which focused around three main attributes: *entertain*, *pamper*, and *empower*. Rather than drive reservations, the campaign's goal was to evoke emotional connections between the brand and travelers in ways that build awareness and consumer loyalty.

The Challenge

The biggest challenge that BLITZ faced was the ability to integrate the traditional campaign look and feel seamlessly into the interactive space that would allow dynamic animations to be created. To deliver the concept of "journey", Y&R created illustrations that utilized "hand-drawn" lines – which naturally led to the requirement to use this style for all interactive iterations and animations. Because more than 100 dynamic animations were going to be needed throughout the experience, BLITZ had to create a drawing engine in Flash that would allow users to trigger different responses through interaction. It was also important that this engine work with the viral, create-a-card effort that was baked into the site.

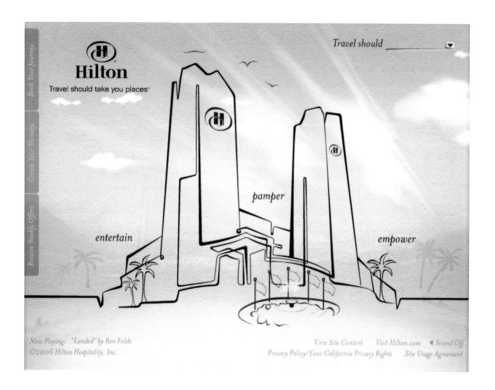

The Solution

Utilizing the stylized key art and a simple color palette, BLITZ created a surreal destination that allowed visitors to "take a break" from their busy day. Through mouse-gesture recognition, users were able to bring the site and story to life within three specific vignettes built around the Hilton Journeys experience: entertain, pamper, and empower. To further enhance the user participation, BLITZ integrated a gesture recognition engine allowing the user to employ a virtual pen to draw shapes recognized by the computer, which then triggered traditionally drawn animation sequences. The engine was especially useful with the viral element, which gave users the chance to customize an animated Hilton Journeys card that could be sent to a friend via email.

The Results

The Hilton Journeys experience turned out to be a great success, drawing an average 15-minute stay time, with nearly every user participating with each part of the journey-based experience. BLITZ was able to use their technical prowess to make the site perform well (in regards to quick loading and smart UI design), but also used their creative muscle to translate the campaign's look and feel into the online space in ways that added relevance and stickiness. The campaign not only changed the perceptions of business travelers, but also recruited a younger audience as well as recreational travelers.

870,000 Site visits

15 Minutes average time on site

53,000 User-generated cards

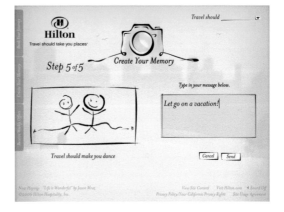

67

Microsoft Realizing Potential

The work Blitz did was phenomenal. Gorgeous visual design. Technologically, it pushed the limits of the medium in the best possible ways. From a content perspective, the storytelling was inviting, and the researcher cameos were truly magical. Altogether it added up to a brand experience that exceeded our goals and expectations across the board."
Jamil Rich, Senior Brand Manager, Microsoft Corporation

The Brief

As Microsoft moved forward with their new, corporate brand positioning – Your Potential. Our Passion. – they were looking to reinvigorate their image as creative and technological pioneers who have never stopped pursuing innovations since their inception. BLITZ was tasked with turning their vision into an online experience that would excite pragmatic consumers and discerning technophiles. The campaign had not only to capture audience analytics, but also to gather unique insights that would allow Microsoft to measure perception shifts among its varying audience groups.

The Challenge

Among a large group of consumers there was a negative perception about Microsoft, a perception that the software giant lacked originality and innovation. The reality, however, was quite the opposite. For years Microsoft had been innovating new ways to help users reach goals and meet their hidden potential.

Client
Microsoft

Credits
BLITZ Agency
www.blitzagency.com

Awards
FWA, Flash Forward, Web Awards, MAX, LA ADDY

www.microsoft.com/about/
brandcampaigns/innovation/
yourpotential/main.html

The Solution
Using the Fabric Flash Framework, which includes toolsets that allow for automated user bandwidth profiling, deep-linking technology, intelligent sound design, and accessibility controls, BLITZ created a branded experience that showcased Microsoft's then-current and future innovations, all of which highlighted the positive effects Microsoft technology has on consumers' everyday lives. Every element of the experience was finely filmed and crafted by BLITZ, from cameos of Microsoft innovators introducing projects to a moving narrative by actor William H. Macy. To ensure the campaign's success, BLITZ worked closely with the Microsoft team to track brand perceptions through targeted user surveys and a media buy that helped increase site traffic. Over the course of the campaign we made several updates, optimizing performance every step of the way.

The Results
The experience gave visitors a never-before-seen look inside one of the world's most revered companies. The story-driven structure and high production value received high praise at Microsoft, and led to new partnerships on several other important initiatives. One of the most impressive aspects of the project was the end-user survey results, showing the campaign's success in increasing positive perceptions of the brand by 12%.

5
—
Minutes average
time on site

12
—
Percent change in
positive perception

70
—
Percent returning
visitors

The Heidies
Diesel Intimate Collection

"I am dying. This is beyond anything I have seen before! You are all so cool."
Janet, site visitor

The Brief

Create an integrated online marketing campaign to drive awareness of Diesel's newly launched intimate collection. Deliver a brand building experience and establish an intimate dialogue with the consumer.

The Challenge

To drive awareness of the intimate collection beyond regular Diesel.com site visitors, by reaching as wide an international audience, in as cost-effective means as possible. Deliver as much traffic to Diesel.com as possible. Create an engaging, sexy, and unconventional experience that would appeal to the young and young-minded.

Client
Diesel

Credits
Diesel Creative Team
www.diesel.com
Farfar
www.farfar.se

Awards
Cannes, Epica, Clio, LIA, Webby

Campaigns
The Heidies
Diesel Intimate Collection

The Solution

Two gorgeous and crazy girls stole the new Diesel Intimate collection, kidnapped a nice guy, locked themselves (and him) in a hotel room. While wearing Diesel Underwear all the time the Heidies broadcast themselves via six video cameras, 24 hours a day, live for five straight days on Diesel.com, which they had hijacked. They went on to get more than their 15 MB of fame, as a live, unscripted, 100% uncensored, interactive story unfolded.

Visitors influenced the direction of the action by sending in emails, voting on polls, and by posting via an uncensored message board on the Diesel homepage. These were fed live to a giant TV screen in the girls' hotel room, giving visitors instant feedback that the event was live, and giving them the chance to interact directly with the Heidies.

The solution was unique as it proposed to invest the project's entire budget into the creation of an event without spending anything on media. The solution was one of the first to embrace social media, posting videos and images to YouTube, MySpace, and Flickr accounts, that drove additional visibility. Videos hosted on YouTube were placed on Diesel.com leveraging the Diesel site's traffic to bump up the video rankings in YouTube.

The Results

An overwhelming success from all angles! Over five days, more than 500,000 unique visitors interacted directly with the campaign on Diesel.com, 300,000 of which can be attributed directly to the viral spread of the online buzz across the Web. Doubling the average weekly traffic to Diesel.com, and at its peak reaching three times the daily average, this was all achieved without any media or seeding investment.

Awareness of the new collection reached an even wider audience, via buzz across the Web, including mentions on 2,400 blogs, news, and fashion sites, and articles on TV and radio. Users returned daily, and interacted for even hours at a time. Over 200,000 messages were posted, and thousands of comments left. The girls made 100s of friends, many of whom begged for the site not to be shut down at the end of the campaign. The event generated 100s of adrenalin-fuelled images taken by the girls themselves, that spread across the Web, some of which being used subsequently in a print campaign.

500,000
Unique users (over 5 days)

2,400
Times blogged

200,000
Messages posted

3
Times daily traffic at Diesel.com

Ford Fusion Mixer

"The success of the Ford Fusion Mixer can be summed up in one number: 90%. That's the percentage of registered Mixer users who opted in to receive future communications about the Ford Fusion – several times the industry average – in exchange for little else than a truly engaging, relevant and innovative interactive experience."
Andres Fernandez, Creative Supervisor for Integrated Marketing, Zubi Advertising

The Brief
AgencyNet was tasked with creating a viral initiative for the Ford Fusion. The Ford Fusion is a unique vehicle in its class, a fusion of a sporty interior with a classic, sleek Ford Sedan exterior all backed by Ford engineering. The target demographic was a unique blend as well – Hispanic Americans, Asian Americans, and African Americans. An analogy was drawn between the well-rounded vehicle and the fusion of music the Fusion Mixer enabled.

The Challenge
AgencyNet's challenge was to provide consumers with an engaging experience that creatively articulated the unique attributes of the Ford Fusion. Ford also needed the ability to reach multiple demographics via a single execution. The vehicle is a wonderful synthesis of modern engineering, technical innovation, and comfort. The deployment needed to convey that sense of automotive fusion while targeting a wide audience profile. The technical and auditory challenge of merging multiple musical genres (often with distinct speeds and conflicting beat counts) into a single mix that truly harmonized was an incredibly difficult outcome to achieve.

Client
Ford Fusion

Credits
AgencyNet
www.agencynet.com

http://fordfusionmixer.agencynet.com

The Solution

AgencyNet created the Ford Fusion Mixer to take advantage of fusing (mixing) together various distinct genres of world music including Alternative, Country, Hip-Hop, Rock, R&B, Reggaeton, Salsa, and Tango. Each genre is broken down into rhythm, harmony, melody, lead, and arrangement channels, each becoming one channel within the five-channel mixer.

This approach is unique within the online mixer realm, as it allows users to mix together synchronously five distinct genres of music and to make changes to their music on the fly – making every mix unique. By combining five genres with five channels, users have the ability to create an unlimited number of unique mixes and are encouraged to explore the distinctive harmonious sounds produced by combining their selected genres. A viral component gives users the opportunity to save and share mixes with friends. Throughout the experience, the Fusion Mixer continually draws the creative analogy of fusing cultures, music, and the Fusion vehicle; a mix of sporty, functional, and classic automotive engineering.

The Results

The result is an eye-popping site that blends music and design in a way that keeps the consumer's attention longer than any 30-second spot could.

The site targets upwardly mobile Generation X consumers whose tastes in music and technology influenced Ford's entire Fusion marketing campaign. The site is so engaging that Fusion Mixer users opt in to receive more information about Fusion at an unprecedented rate of almost 90%.

90 — Percent opt-in rate

37,500 — Google results

10 — Minutes average time on site

Bacardi DJ

"Bacardi DJ is a true testament to how a brand can provide an engaging consumer experience to create a distinctive brand aura that extends beyond its product attributes."
Richard McLeod, Senior Brand Manager, Bacardi Superior Rum

The Brief

AgencyNet was asked to create an innovative, and addicting digital music mixer. Bacardi DJ was an extension of Bacardi's music platform, which is a key part of Bacardi's marketing message. Bacardi DJ gave aspiring DJs of any skill level the chance to mix and produce their own unique tracks. It was designed for anyone who wanted to learn a new skill or be discovered. The tool was very easy to use and provided consumers with a lot of fun in the process. AgencyNet wanted to take it a step further and allow users to download tracks to their iPods, taking brand interaction on the road.

The Challenge

Over a five-year campaign duration, AgencyNet was consistently challenged to enhance the sophisticated, sleek aesthetic of Bacardi DJ. Each iteration of the site included more loops than the previous time, a fresh consumer campaign, and technical enhancements like downloadable MP3s of user-made mixes.

Client
Bacardi Global Brands

Credits
AgencyNet
www.agencynet.com

Awards
FWA, IMA, SoFIE, Webby, Davey

www.bacardidj.com

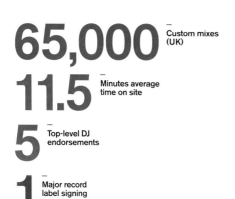

65,000 Custom mixes (UK)

11.5 Minutes average time on site

5 Top-level DJ endorsements

1 Major record label signing

The Solution

Throughout the campaign, over seven hundred custom loops were created specifically for Bacardi DJ, creating an extensive loop library for users. Five genres of loops lead to the complexity of the mixer and the mixes themselves. The mixer's core functionality was also enhanced in order to give users greater flexibility to create unique mixes, including master (cross-channel) volume functionality. Additionally a groundbreaking conversion tool was developed, allowing users to convert their tracks to MP3. This one-of-a-kind function allowed users to save their mix to their computer and MP3 player, providing not only portability for Bacardi DJ, but added brand-interaction time as well.

The Results

The impact of the project amplified over its five-year duration. In addition to an average brand-interaction time of 11.5 minutes, the site gained instant credibility by being endorsed by top-level, professional DJs Carl Cox, Krafty Kuts, Lisa Pin-Up, Shortee Blitz and DJ Bailey. The overall judging panel for the contest included an MTV VJ, an MTV Music Editor, a Universal Records executive, and the founder of Dusted Clothing.

The dynamic buzz campaign garnered dozens of online awards including FWA Site of the Day and a myriad of traditional awards such as the Interactive Media Award for Best in Class. The site achieved even more recognition when it was featured in TASCHEN's Web Design: Music Sites book.

Beaches Send-a-Sandcastle

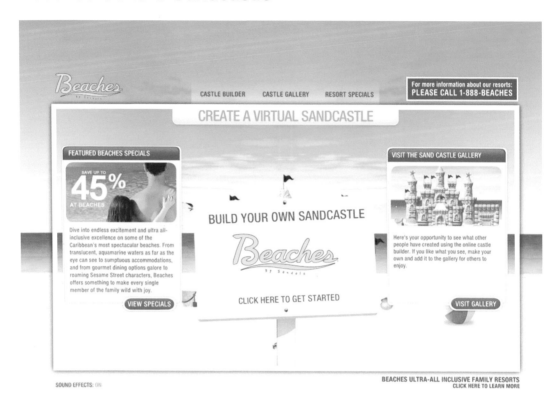

"Virtual Sandcastle gave us a great opportunity to create a collaborative experience that encouraged parents to create with their children. Our hope was to get them to sit together and enjoy the creative process together just as they would when they eventually visited a Beaches family Resort."
Garett Bugda, Executive Creative Director

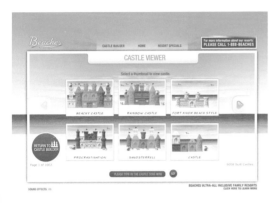

The Brief

Beaches is the ultimate chain of all-inclusive family vacation resorts in the Caribbean. During peak periods (school vacations, summer break, and Christmas) they do an excellent job of attracting families to their resorts.

In this case, Beaches came to AgencyNet looking to drive sales of family vacations year-round, especially during the slower seasons. Their goal was to target families with pre-school age children so that vacation schedules were not dictated exclusively by the school calendar. Additionally, it was requested that the initiative be playable and encourage sharing within the family... all the while embodying that "perfect, family vacation" that Beaches provides.

The Challenge

To introduce vacation decision-makers to Beaches Resorts' family-friendly resort properties and educate them on each resort's distinctive personality. The experience would ultimately need to drive users to the booking engine.

Beaches Resorts' most profitable times of the year are during academic breaks: winter break, summer break, and spring break. The objective of this campaign was to attract families with small children who were not yet enrolled in school through a holistic campaign, to increase bookings at non-peak times of the year.

Client
Beaches Resorts

Credits
AgencyNet
www.agencynet.com

Awards
IMA

www.virtualsandcastle.com

The Solution

By focusing on Beaches Resorts' brand essence of togetherness and family interaction, AgencyNet identified sandcastles as an icon representative of family bond-building. The activity was indicative of how our target demo envisioned their perfect family escape.

The Send-a-Sandcastle application utilizes familiar "plastic castle molds" for users to build their own digital sandcastle and send it to their loved ones. The application was simple to use, yet incorporated enough advanced functionality to allow for more intricate designs. Users also select a beach backdrop for their sandcastle from images of Beaches resorts, thus introducing visitors to the various properties.

The Results

The site boasts an average brand-interaction time of 19 minutes for castle builders. Limited to a blog-only marketing campaign, the site has over 400 known blog posts linking to VirtualSandcastle.com. The user-generated sandcastle gallery has grown to over 6,011 castles with 50% of the castles sent to a friend, generating unique visits to the site.

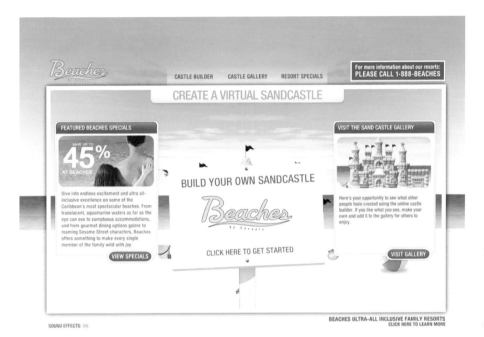

17.54 Minutes average time on site

6,011 Sandcastles built

400 Blog posts

22.41 Hours longest interaction

Get the Glass

"I became obsessed with getting the glass and kept getting sent to Milkatraz. Get the Glass was funny, well executed, highly playable, ridiculously sticky and hit multiple product message points. Definitely the cream of a great crop."
Jonah Bloom, Advertising Age, USA

Client
The California Milk Processor Board

Credits
Goodby, Silverstein & Partners
www.goodbysilverstein.com
North Kingdom
www.northkingdom.com

Awards
Cannes, FWA, Flashforward, LIA, HOW, ADC, LD&AD, Clios, New York Festivals, Webby, One Show, Future Marketing, Mediaweek, Comm Arts

www.gettheglass.com

The Brief

"Got milk?" is Goodby, Silverstein & Partners' oldest account, dating back to 1993. For 12 years, up until 2005, we'd advertised this most traditional of products in the most traditional of mediums: television.

But even though milk hadn't changed since 1993, the world around it had. By 2005, most Californians were online. In addition, they were leading the nation in adoption of DVRs – devices that pose challenges to getting our traditional TV ads seen. And lastly, the "super-drink" strategy we shifted to in late 2005 focused on educating people about the wide range of specific benefits milk delivers – muscle rebuilding and stronger hair, nails, teeth, etc. We wanted to use online to engage with consumers outside of TV and tell them about milk's many benefits in a highly entertaining way.

The Challenge

We had created a television campaign that told the story of a family deprived of milk on a quest to "get the glass." The family believed the glass of milk would help them with their ailments – weak hair, weak muscles, weak nails, cavity-riddled teeth, and frequent bouts of PMS. Our challenge was to take this story online and engage others in this quest. We needed to come up with a creative device where people could interact with the family's story but also learn about the benefits of milk. We needed to make it fun for everyone to "Get the Glass."

4.5 Million total visits

9 Minutes average
time on site

28 Million page views

2,305 Blogs linking to
gettheglass.com

The Solution

If we wanted people to experience this family's quest to get the glass, why not create a game built around the premise? It had to be a game that didn't get too complicated. That's what led us to a game style most everyone is familiar with already: the classic board-game. Except our board-game lives online and users could actually win a real glass sent to their home.

All users had to do was roll the dice and they were off. The game was filled with familiar conventions that reinforced the health benefits of milk. Some of those conventions included multiple-choice questions; others were fully interactive game challenges. The users had three chances to try to get the glass or else they would be permanently sent to Milkatraz.

The Results

Gettheglass.com succeeded beyond our wildest imaginations. The site attracted more than 3,505,385 unique visitors who stayed and played for an average of nine minutes!

An exit survey showed that people were learning about all the specific benefits milk offers and found that 80% of visitors said they wanted to come back and play again.

Our tracking study showed that people who'd experienced the campaign online strongly associated milk with all the key benefits we communicated and rated milk much higher on attributes like "milk is nature's super-drink," "it's unique," "it's what strong and healthy people drink."

Estudio Coca-Cola Zero

"This Coke Zero online music program
was developed to fit perfectly the brand's
needs, and the results were amazing. We
engaged users in our message using a
combination of relevant content, relevant
applications and relevant distribution."
Adriana Knackfuss, Interactive Marketing
Manager, Coca-Cola Brazil

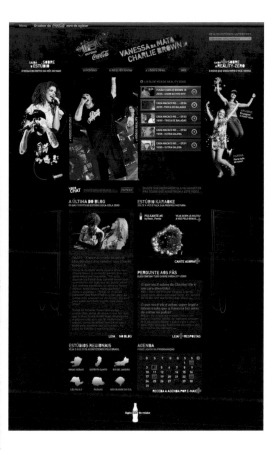

The Brief

Develop the new Coke Zero online music platform in Brazil and create solid engagement with users through high-frequency impact and content co-creation through the development of the content and brand message.

Leverage the concept of the studio on the Web: two directly opposite musical style bands will join once a month in a show televised to Brazilian audiences. The campaign lasts for four months, so four band groups are to be showcased.

The Challenge

How to engage a massive audience and keep the interest in the content high and continuous through four months of campaign and recruit more than the regular share of fans of each of the participating bands?

Agencies included in the campaign: Gringo (overall strategy and production), JWT (online media), Riot (social media strategy and execution).

Client
Coca-Cola

Credits
Gringo
www.gringo.nu
JWT Brazil
www.jwt.com.br
Riot
www.riot.com.br

Awards
Wave Festival 08 – Brazil

The Solution

Other than giving asynchronous visibility to all the content produced for TV on the website, we extracted the core mechanics of the campaign (band A versus band B, creating an interesting musical tension and curiosity) and brought this to everyday life through the creation of exclusive and new online content.

Every month we followed closely the lives of two fans who agreed to change places with their opposite (Country/Heavy Metal, for instance), complete with visual makeover, exposure to family and friends circles, and frequenting each other's clubs and events. Each misadventure was captured on film as a four-minute documentary aired every other day only on the Web and digital channels, complete with each character's on-the-fly twittering their every move, frustrations, and discoveries.

Users were able to choose the next-day challenges faced by our unlikely heroes through a voting process online. We also created an online karaoke, where users were able to experience the Coke Zero musical fusion by themselves.

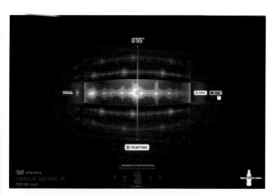

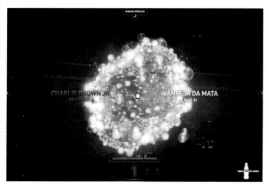

The Results

The campaign achieved unprecedented results, impacting 96% of all Internet users in Brazil. Coca-Cola was able to establish the music platform with success within its new Zero brand, allowing users to interact with the content and create their very own and share with the world. It has been the most successful Coke Zero campaign to date, and the campaign with the highest reach Coca-Cola has launched in the Brazilian market.

43.9 Million unique users

26 Communities created

3.8 Million YouTube views

3 Million people impacted by social communities

Robo Brawl

"This little gem definitely takes the cake as "site of the month". RoboBrawl, promotional minisite for Intel Xeon, is very well executed on so many fronts – user experience, design, illustration, typography, animation, usability, sound, music... it's the total package."
BLOGNA.org

Client
Intel

Credits
Godfrey Q and Partners
www.gqpsf.com

RED Interactive Agency
www.ff0000.com

Awards
FWA, FITC, WebAward

http://robo.ff0000.com

The Brief

The goal of this campaign was to introduce the new Intel Xeon Processor to the gaming audience through a fun, interactive game experience. In Robo Brawl, users could create their own robots and brawl against others, with all robots being powered by the Xeon Processor. The game was playable in both a single-player and multi-player version and amassed a dedicated group of followers that lit up the leaderboard.

The Challenge

The main challenge was coming up with a concept and game logic that could seamlessly integrate the Xeon Processor brand message into the game experience. We needed to show both overtly and metaphorically how the Xeon Processor could increase energy efficiency, virtualization, and performance. It was critical to deliver this brand message while keeping the game fun and exciting. The goal is for the game never to feel like "advertising".

The Solution

The solution was to create a game where each "Robo Brawl" was entertaining enough to warrant repeated plays and site visits. Each robot was powered by the Xeon processor, so as your robot improved, so did your perception of the Xeon's capabilities. Following is an overview of how the game play worked.

Each user started by creating a robot. They used their allotted power-points to access weapons, armor, and transport. Once the user builds their robot, they enter the ring and fight against five other robots. The last one standing is the winner. As users continue to play and win, they amass points which allow them to buy more advanced gear (which was not accessible during the beginning stages of the game). In addition, players start accumulating powerboost points, which increases their energy efficiency, virtualization, and performance.

The Results

The results of the Robo Brawl campaign exceeded expectations. Almost half of all game players came back for more with the top players engaging in almost 2,000 battles.

43 Percent return viewers

30 Percent registrations

20 Average battles played

2,000 Battles by top players

NOLAF (National Organization for Legislation Against Fun)

"I love this site! I have spent a lot of time laughing out loud at my computer when I should be studying. The interaction is great, and the lead guy is hilarious. I have sent it to all my friends."
Sconner1, site visitor

The Brief

Tostitos are enjoyed in social situations, when friends are having fun: the big game, a backyard bbq, a reunion. We need to remind our audience when to buy Tostitos – reinforce that Tostitos are about fun, good times, and socializing.

Tostitos Research, provided by Frito-Lay, showed that their young target audience had a propensity to be active and participate online. However, the communication created in this space for the brand was primarily the same old banner and microsite campaigns. How can Tostitos break through online and create something uniquely different? And, how can this be done without the use of traditional media? Through an engaging viral campaign without the support of traditional media.

The Challenge

Tostitos had a daunting challenge. They wanted to get their tortilla chip to appeal to an entirely new and different target demographic, the 25-35-year-old heavy social snackers. Traditionally the Tostitos corn chip had been perceived as boring and stuffy by the target demographic, and largely overlooked in favor of edgier competitors such as Doritos. So how do you combat this? Well, simple: you take the stuffiness out of the brand by thinking entirely outside of the box and reimagining the brand as one that is fun, wacky, unexpected, and willing to take a risk. Make Tostitos fun in the most unexpected way possible.

Client
Frito-Lay

Credits
Mekanism
www.mekanism.com
Element 79
www.Element79.com

Awards
FWA, One Show, Addy, D&AD

http://nolaf.mekanism.com

101

The Solution

We developed an online buzz campaign about a fictional organization, NOLAF (the National Organization for Legislation Against Fun). The center of the campaign is a full-screen video site showcasing NOLAF and their crusade against all things fun, especially the pleasure of eating Tostitos. The shorts include lectures and Q&A sessions with seven hopeful NOLAF members – totaling over an hour of interactive content. In devolving the characters we wanted to poke fun at recognizable groups of boring people without being cruel. We wanted our audience to immediately recognize the people we parodied, without resorting to stereotypes. In the end, we did exactly what Tostitos had been asking for: we took the word *boring* away from the brand and created an edgier, surprising destination that was fun and unexpected.

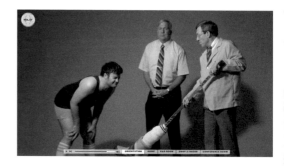

300,000 — Site visits

4 — Million views on YouTube

#1 — Most-viewed channel on YouTube

#3 — Most-viewed video on YouTube

The Results

All of the traffic was driven to the site entirely through non-traditional outreach. Basically put: we had nothing. So we let our content syndication program build awareness for the campaign by seeding and promoting 20 NOLAF viral videos on over 50 user-generated content sites (such as YouTube, Break, and Heavy), 20 social bookmarking sites (such as digg and stumbleupon) and outreach to hundreds of blogs and digital influencers.

NOLAF became an overwhelming success. Our use of social media – promoting NOLAF on social bookmarking sites, seeding and distribution to UGC sites, in conjunction with bloggers and influencers, created a powerful viral launch pad. This "network effect" generated over four million video views – with zero dollars spent in traditional media. Not too shabby.

The Fixers

"Sex-fueled and witty, the Axe
Fixers campaign does an
excellent job of reminding its
customers why it is the best
shower gel on the market."
beatskate.com

Client
Axe/Unilever

Credits
Mekanism
www.mekanism.com

Awards
FWA

www.thefixers.com

The Brief

We were given the task of launching a new line of shower gels for Axe that consisted of four variants – Shock, Fever, Snake Peel, and Recovery – with each one designed to give guys the edge in the mating game. Our job was to communicate the unique transformational benefits of each gel to 18-24-year-old guys, and in the process to nudge the whole Axe brand forward a bit, away from acting as an aphrodisiac for women, and instead, acting as an agent of change on the guys themselves: something that makes them feel better when they use it.

The Challenge

The challenge of this campaign was to reach young men in the increasingly shifting media landscape, and communicate to them the nuances and benefits of four different shower gels knowing full well that guys don't talk to other guys about showering and hygiene and soap. What we needed was a platform that simultaneously educated them, appealed to their mating-game concerns, and gave them the tools to share this new knowledge with their friends.

The Solution

The solution? Pranks guys could play on each other that revolved around the transformational power of the Fixer line, without ever getting too creepy and personal. And to host the pranks, TheFixers.com – a full-screen, live-action talk show with funny instructional segments, and the digital pranking system to help concerned friends rehabilitate buddies in need of a game makeover.

The online talk show features a real-life problem solver named "The Fixer" who explored the difficulties guys often face in their demanding social lives. Covering everything from questionable social behaviour to minimizing party recovery time, the online episodes culminated in a series of interactive pranks designed to teach valuable lessons and offer solutions to keep every guy up and running. By creating content that appeals entirely to that of the core demographic, we allowed it to be a vessel for on-point, peer-to-peer brand messaging.

The Results

For starters, a lot of guys pranking guys. But more importantly, The Fixers site and campaign were overwhelmingly successful. The site itself garnered nearly a million unique visitors, and engagement was extremely high – the average time spent was nearly five minutes per user. Furthermore, the content was embraced by bloggers, and videos from The Fixers site and commercial garnered over three million views on YouTube and other User-Generated Content sites. We started with the basic truth that guys don't talk to their friends about hygiene the way girls do, but instead use pranks and humor to educate each other, and ended with an engaging and funny Web experience that crossed platforms and got the target excited about shower gel.

1
Million site visits

5
Minutes average time on site

3
Million views on UGC sites

E-Commerce

Introduction by
Alex Bogusky, Crispin Porter + Bogusky

commerce

"An analysis of the history of technology shows that technological change is exponential, contrary to the common-sense 'intuitive linear' view. So we won't experience 100 years of progress in the 21st century – it will be more like 20,000 years of progress (at today's rate)." – Raymond Kurzweil

Raymond doesn't work in advertising, but if he did, he would be very excited about the future of e-commerce. We are in the very infancy of the category, and the future is probably beyond what most of us can imagine now.

"With all this 'e'commerce going on, we're working up a big appetite; good thing we can now buy our favorite custom pizza with the push of a button, and watch as it's made, boxed, and sent on its way to our front door."

To explain the exponential change about to occur, Ray tells the story of the Chinese emperor who so loved the game of chess that he offered the inventor a reward for its creation. The inventor asked for a single grain of rice for the first square on the board, two grains for the second, four for the third, and so on. The emperor quickly agreed, excited to get off so cheaply. They went through the first half of the chessboard without too much trouble; the inventor was given spoonfuls, then bowls, and soon whole wagonloads of rice. By the end of the first half of the board, the inventor had accumulated one large field of rice, and the emperor began to realize he had struck a very expensive deal. If they had continued across the rest of the board, by the end, there would not have been enough land-mass on all the earth to supply the rice that the inventor was owed. Legend has it that he was soon executed as a reward for his extreme cleverness.

Nice story about rice, but what about "e"commerce? Well, if we take a look at our current computer technology, we're basically halfway through the chessboard; there have been approximately 32 doublings since the first computers were invented during World War II.

"E"commerce can loosely be considered any use of electronic technology to make a transaction. So it's been around for a while – but it continues to get more exciting as the Web and computer technologies improve and the adoption increases. Over and over, categories that were deemed impenetrable by "e"commerce have fallen, Zappos and shoe sales being the most famous recent example, but I remember people being skeptical about online clothing sales in general.

And now, we can have groceries delivered to our house – or we can sell our house; we can sell the crap we found in the basement last summer – or we can purchase a prefab addition to add a new bedroom to our house. With all this "e"commerce going on, we're working up a big appetite; good thing we can now buy our favorite custom pizza with the push of a button, and watch as it's made, boxed, and sent on its way to our front door.

"The very term 'e'commerce has certainly become outdated, specifically when you look at it from the consumer's point of view."

The very term "e"commerce has certainly become outdated, specifically when you look at it from the consumer's point of view. They don't make a distinction any more. It isn't special or extraordinary. It's just called buying or shopping, and it's part of the same behavior as driving to the mall. The consumer also has a set of expectations for "e"commerce transactions and experiences that are just as high as, or sometimes higher than, the expectations for their physical transactions. So if the consumer has stopped differentiating, why is it that retailers and marketers are still making distinctions?

The vast majority of organizations we deal with usually have separate divisions that handle the digital transactions. In many cases, they are even entirely separate companies; each senior management team runs separate agendas and day-to-day business, with no incentive to see the whole picture, or to create a seamless experience for the consumer. This leads to disjointed and disconnected brand expressions, and therefore consumer experiences. And innovations in selling, or merchandising, that could have benefits for the entire organization are stuck in one silo or the other. All this legacy structure that was once built to implement "e"commerce has become in many cases the very thing that limits it now. It's successful. It works. The limitations are no longer with the technology. The only obstacle left is how integrated and imaginative we can be in bringing great buying experiences to the consumer.

As digital media was birthed, it was often referred to as "alternative" media, and today a lot of people still refer to it as such. Well, if you use the term "alternative", you are certainly missing the reality of today's economic culture, and really missing a lot of opportunity. If you want to be successful today, it's simply not an alternative. In fact, it's pretty damn mandatory. When the term "alternative" media is thrown out in our office, people immediately apologize – or face a lot of teasing. I think this reaction is an important part of how an organization can help itself move forward and think progressively.

So, in my opinion, the first and most important step in thinking about the future of e-commerce is easy: Lose the "e".

Alex Bogusky
Crispin Porter + Bogusky

Bio.
<u>Alex Bogusky</u>
Crispin Porter + Bogusky

Alex joined Crispin and Porter Advertising in 1989 as an art director. He became the creative director five years later, a partner in 1997, and co-chairman in 2008. Under Alex's direction, Crispin Porter + Bogusky has grown to include more than 900 employees, with offices in Miami, Boulder, Los Angeles, and London. CP+B has become one of the world's most awarded agencies and is the only agency to have won the Cannes International Advertising Festival Grand Prix in all five categories: Promotion, Media, Cyber, Titanium, and Film.

Alex was inducted into the Art Directors Club Hall of Fame in 2008, and in May of 2009 he received an honorary Ph.D. from the University of Colorado. Most Mondays, he comes to work with at least one bloody, oozing injury that forces people to look away.
–
www.cpbgroup.com

"The first and most important step in thinking about the future of e-commerce is easy: Lose the 'e.'"

Dominos.com

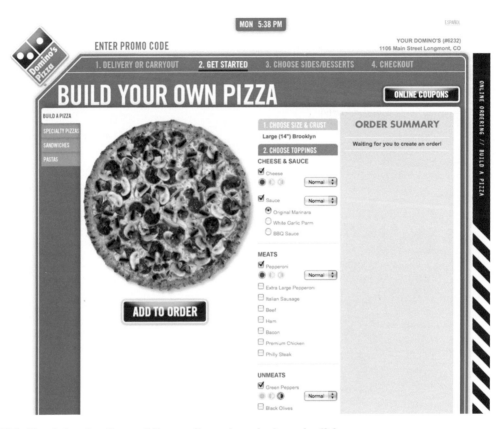

"With the introduction of the online visual pizza builder, Dominos.com has once again raised the bar for online food ordering. Our customers love watching their creation come to life, and the instant visual feedback of topping selections helps reduce ordering errors. A win-win for customers and our organization alike."
Rob Weisberg, VP, Precision & Print Marketing

The Brief

In 2006, Domino's launched their online ordering platform and was last in the category to get to market. They needed to close the gap quickly, and asked the agency to develop a strategic plan that would enable them to hit their aggressive online sales goals, identify new digital sales, marketing, and innovation opportunities, new audiences, and differentiate their shopping experience.

The Challenge

We knew the online ordering system would be the frontline in our battle to better the competition. In our research, we found the category to be dull, homogeneous, and devoid of brand romance. The process of ordering online was all checks and boxes. We felt it could and should be much more. We saw the redesign as an opportunity to differentiate the brand through development of a shopping platform that brought convenience, utility, and entertainment together in one seamless and memorable experience, making the site both a powerful sales and marketing tool. Our key challenge was adding the brand experience layer without sacrificing our conversion rate and sales goals in the process; a delicate balance to strike when you consider that a misplaced button or slow experience can drastically affect the bottom line.

Client
Dominos

Credits
Crispin Porter + Bogusky
www.cpbgroup.com

Awards
Clios, Cannes, One Show, LIA

www.dominos.com

13 Million orders tracked

100 Percent increase in online orders

113 Quintillion pizza variation possibilities

7 Percent market share increase

8.9 Million Visual Builder pizzas created

ESPAÑOL

LOCAL OFFERINGS

elivery experts at
to date on
aves our
before.

DOMINO'S // PIZZA TRACKER

★★★
★★★
★★★

DOMINO'S.
SEND

The Solution

The most effective way to reach our goals was to become the preferred tool to shop for pizza on the Internet. We set out to do that by developing two ordering tools that would introduce a whole new level of convenience and utility for our user.

The first, Pizza Tracker, became a best-in-class tool that allows users to see the progress of their order in real time during five stages: Order Placed, Prepped, Baked, Boxed, and Out for Delivery. This created unprecedented transparency for the consumer, and tied in with our brand promise: "You Got 30 Minutes".

The second, Visual Builder, allows users a fun and intuitive way to create their pizza order. An animated visual representation of the pizza displays the nearly limitless number of possible pizza crust and topping combinations available, and is accurate down to the store level. This assures users they will never build a pizza they cannot actually order.

The Results

Within 16 months, the creation of the revamped ordering system, and the integration of the online ordering tools resulted in a 70% increase in site visits, while online orders increased 1.5 times. Overall site conversion rate increased in excess of 50% and over 10 million new users registered on Dominos.com. These massive gains ultimately allowed Domino's to move from third in online pizza ordering to first, in terms of market share.

Lowe's Sunnyville

"Sites like this one make you realize that
agencies such as Tribal DDB and Firstborn
are not just churning out projects. Their
passion definitely shines through."
Rob Ford, FWA

Client
Lowe's Home Improvement

Credits
Tribal DDB Worldwide
www.trialddb.com
Firstborn
www.firstbornmultimedia.com

Awards
FWA, One Show, Adobe,
NY Times, SXSW

www.lookwhatwemade.com/
sunnyville_campaign

The Brief

Convince homeowners that Lowe's is their one-stop-shop for everything spring – increased sales, growth of category, interaction with brand. Generate awareness and convey the breadth of their products by letting consumers interact with the products online. Drive traffic and sales, in-store and online, by leading the consumers through the purchase funnel and providing cross-selling opportunities. Build brand affinity by creating an engaging online experience that they will want to keep coming back to.

The Challenge

The challenge was how we would create this immersive video/3-D experience but bring interactive elements to it, allowing users to experience the Lowe's Spring Product line. We still had to make the products the centerpiece of the site, so created a product catalogue that was integrated into the video content throughout the site. We also created the Yard Creator, which let people build their own yard with Lowe's products and see it grow over time.

The Solution
For Lowe's Home Improvement stores, springtime is their holiday season. So to celebrate this most wonderful time of the year, we welcomed people back from hibernation with Sunnyville – a fantastical neighborhood where the weather is almost as perfect as the backyards. Here users can find inspiration by exploring the backyards of each of their quirky neighbors, play with fun tools (like the Meat Calculator), and even use the Yard Creator to build and maintain their own living yard. Along the way, they can find all of Lowe's products and expertise to get out and do spring right.

The Results
During the three-month drive period Sunnyville had: 143,282 total visits; 135,675 unique visitors; 4.27 minutes' average time spent on the site; most popular task was the "Mike the Bear" game.

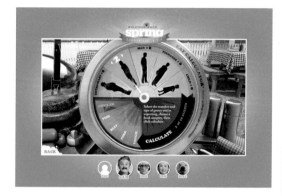

145,000 Site visits

45 Minutes of video on site

250 Products on sale

7 Weeks production time

Ciamillo Components N.E.R.D. Campaign

"The N.E.R.D. campaign was a eureka moment for the company. The results were through the roof! From a marketing standpoint it was one of those 'if you build it, they will come' type scenarios. It accurately anticipated what the people were longing for."
Christian Ries Foster, Director of Sales and Marketing, Ciamillo Components, Inc.

Client
Ciamillo Components, Inc

Credits
Studio Mds
www.studiomds.com

www.studiomds.com/negg

The Brief

Ciamillo Components wanted to develop a limited-edition road brakeset that would commemorate Brian Molloy, the technical consultant who helped make the company's products some of the most coveted high-end components in the cycling industry. Concurrently, Ciamillo wanted to leverage their existing brand to create a one-of-a-kind component that would be highly sought after due to its exclusivity. Most importantly, it needed to exhibit the physical characteristics and proven performance of the Negative G, its model brand, while becoming its own unique limited-edition product.

The Challenge

Creating a comprehensive and effective campaign from top to bottom in just a few days was the biggest challenge. The basis for the brakeset was in existence as a part of the standard product line, but there were no other assets to leverage. A large number of creative solutions needed to be generated in a very short amount of time in order to satisfy the company's desire to launch the campaign as quickly as possible. There was not a clear direction on the campaign given by the client other than to "come up with something cool". The name, price, and quantity of the limited-edition brakeset were all to be determined.

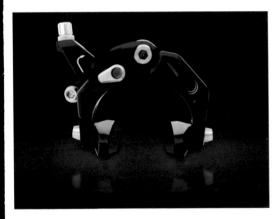

Ciamillo Components N.E.R.D. Campaign

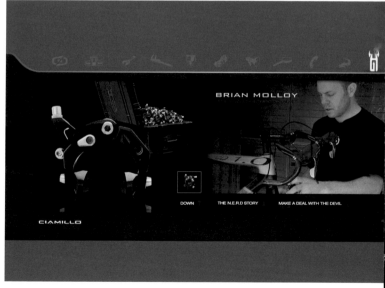

The Solution

The answer lay in the inspiration for the limited edition: Brian Molloy… aka the New England Devil. By adding an "R" for the bold red color of the product, the pseudonym became an acronym and a theme was born: The N.E.R.D. The acronym suggested "the brains" behind the product's engineering while the "Devil" and associated branding effectively *tempted* the consumer to investigate further. The price and quantity were aptly positioned at 666. A fresh logo was designed to be used as the exclusive brand for this new limited-edition brakeset. Believable Photoshop renditions of a non-existent product were developed. A lo-fi promotional, comedic short was storyboarded, shot, and edited inside of 24 hours. All facets of the campaign were seamlessly integrated into a powerful and engaging user experience. Finally, online ads were created to drive traffic to the new campaign.

The Results

Within days of launching the campaign all 666 sets were completely sold out. Priced at $666 per set, the campaign resulted in radical profit generation for the small company (less than ten employees). The cycling industry was blown away with the visual appeal of the new red anodized product, which was previously only available in black. With this being the most successful marketing campaign to date, Ciamillo Components was forced to restructure its production process for the welcomed spike in demand. The success of the N.E.R.D. and the commensurate confidence that was inspired, spawned the company's current custom brake-building program.

5 Days to design and develop

666 Sets sold in less than a week

443,556 U.S. dollars gross profit

Adobe CS3 Product Selector Tool

"The Adobe Product Selector Tool was a leap forward in the way Adobe uses the Web to provide contextual, information-rich decision tools to our customers. The Product Selector had a tremendous impact on the way users evaluated upgrades and purchases of the CS3 products, and its effectiveness was fueled by a simple, elegant and functional design. Without the experience, design and technical know-how that BLITZ provided on this project, the Product Selector would never have come to life."
AJ Joseph, Creative Director, Adobe Systems, Inc.

Client
Adobe

Credits
BLITZ Agency
www.blitzagency.com

Awards
LA ADDY

http://www.blitzagency.com/
ourWork.aspx?project=
69&template=cs

The Brief
In 2007, Adobe introduced Creative Suite 3, a software bundle that included up to 13 different applications for cross platform designers and developers. It was the largest product launch in their 25-year history. That said, they needed a solution that would easily allow designers and developers to find the best possible bundle based on their needs. And not only was this selector going to be utilized within Adobe's own site, it had to be created in a way that allowed Value-added Resellers (VARs) to easily integrate it into their own commerce-based destinations.

The Challenge
Adobe had traditionally used their vast amount of "features" to market their suites. However, with so many new additions to the software, the process of determining the right bundle could seem daunting. Rather than focusing on features, BLITZ created a simple, elegant, streamlined interface that homed in on specific user profiles. In addition, Adobe required the recommendation engine to be externalized in an XML file so they could make adjustments to the recommendations based on their learning of how the tool is actually used by their audience. The user interface had to appeal to a wide audience – from the creative designers, to technical developers and business owners.

668,000
Participants

68
Percent lead
generation

11
Languages
deployed

The Solution
Using Flash and XML, BLITZ developed a
Rich Internet Application that dramatically
simplified the shopping experience through
clarity, honesty, and speed. With a few simple
clicks, users were able to find their bundle,
receive upgrade options and download the trial
online. Not only was the application designed
to live on Adobe's site, it was also utilized by
VARs and Adobe sales teams, and localized
in six languages. The product selector clearly
communicated what software is included in
the product suite and the value of the bundle.
For existing customers, the recommendation
engine demonstrates the best upgrade path
from your current software ownership.

The Results
Since its launch, the CS3 Product Selector
has become the most effective lead-to-sale
tool in Adobe's history. In its first three months
the application received approximately
668,000 unique visits – excluding VARs and
external sales teams – resulting in 68% trial
downloads.

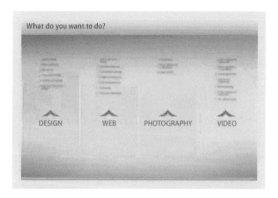

We recommend

Upgrade options | Compare products

What do you want to do?

Inside

- Adobe InDesign CS3
- Adobe Photoshop CS3 Extended
- Adobe Illustrator CS3
- Adobe Acrobat 8 Professional
- Adobe Flash CS3 Professional
- Adobe Dreamweaver CS3
- Adobe Fireworks CS3
- Adobe Contribute CS3
- Adobe After Effects CS3 Professional
- Adobe Premiere Pro CS3
- Adobe Soundbooth CS3
- Adobe Encore CS3
- Adobe Bridge CS3
- Adobe Version Cue CS3

Adobe Creative Suite 3 Master Collection is for those who don't recognize boundaries. A comprehensive creative environment featuring highly integrated tools that support print, web, interactive, film, video, and mobile output, Master Collection is a value-packed offering that helps you meet deadlines while exploring and expressing your creative vision.

Master Collection features highly integrated, all-new versions of professional design, web, and video tools from Adobe. It combines the best of Creative Suite 3 Design Premium, Web Premium, and Production Premium with productivity features that let you produce content for virtually all media.

Learn more

More...

We recommend

Upgrade options | Compare products

What do you want to do?

Look inside

ADOBE AFTER EFFECTS CS3 PROFESSIONAL

Buy US$999

Adobe After Effects CS3 Professional
helps you bring visual effects and motion graphics to life in film, video, DVD, the web, and mobile devices.

Preorder | Notify | Learn more

Inside

- Adobe After Effects CS3 Professional
- Adobe Premiere Pro CS3
- Adobe Photoshop CS3 Extended
- Adobe Flash CS3 Professional
- Adobe Illustrator CS3
- Adobe Soundbooth CS3
- Adobe Encore CS3
- Adobe Bridge CS3
- Adobe Dynamic Link
- Adobe Device Central CS3
- Adobe Acrobat Connect

Plus:
- Adobe OnLocation CS3 (Windows only)
- Adobe Ultra CS3 (Windows only)

Preorder | Notify | Learn more

Style Lounge
Diesel Online Store

"I have always dreamed of a store where all
my favorite products are available at the same
time! Finally, creating a digital gallery, we
provide Diesel fans around the world with a
unique mind-blowing experience of shopping."
Renzo Rosso, Diesel President & Founder

Client
Diesel

Credits
Diesel Creative Team
www.diesel.com
Dvein
www.dvein.com
Neue Digitale
www.neue-digitale.de
wysiwyg* software design
www.wysiwyg.de
Yoox
www.yoox.com

Awards
FWA, Red Dot, Golden Drum,
ADC, Annual Multimedia Award,
The Cup, NYFestivals

www.neue-digitale.de/projects/
diesel_stylelounge

The Brief

Diesel were to launch a new international online store. It would have the largest offering of any single Diesel store, with more than 1,500 different products, three times more than in the average store. Aimed at the more forward-thinking consumer, it would cover the most important collection lines, including specialist denim and items that previously could be found in only a handful of stores worldwide.

With such a wide and frequently changing inventory, presented in five languages to an international audience, the site design was principally focused on functionality and usability. While different motivations may drive the purchase of clothing online, compared with those made in a high-street store, the emotional experience of shopping in a Diesel store is considered a very important aspect in the way customers build their relationship with the brand. It was deemed important that this aspect be translated into the online experience, also helping to differentiate the online store from those of competitor brands.

Diesel first ventured into e-commerce in 1997, as the first major fashion brand to sell its collection online, through its online store in the UK. The experiment was a huge success and demonstrated the potential of online sales. By 2007, after a few years' break from selling online, and while preparing for an international e-commerce launch, Diesel needed to drive awareness of the new store with something special. By then having an online store was no longer a newsworthy story.

The brief was to create a digital "window" for the new Diesel online store that would attract PR and online attention to pull people into the store; to engage the user in an emotional experience that would communicate the creative theme of the collection; at the same time presenting the key styling concepts and key seasonal outfits.

The Challenge

The solution would have to consider how the principles of a store window could translate and evolve to exploit the potential of interactive media. It would need to grab attention, both on- and off-line, and drive traffic to the site. The solution would have to astound and engage without interfering with the overall effectiveness of the main online store.

Diesel products are distinguished by their attention to detail, treatments, and fabrics. The site would have to overcome the challenges of the customer not being able physically to touch the products, by presenting them in as optimal a way as possible. The site would also have to meet raised expectations, as the collection had previously been introduced to the press in the form of a ground-breaking holographic fashion show.

The Solution

The solution invited the user to explore a mysterious underwater world where interactive full-screen video sequences and animations brought the "Liquid Space" collection theme to life, and allowed users to discover the key seasonal outfits. Using footage taken from Diesel's previous holographic fashion show, combined with specially shot video, the fully immersive, three-dimensional experience employed rich interactive animation and lighting effects, combined with an ethereal soundscape, to achieve an overall effect that literally immersed the user in the collection.

Users could navigate freely between different zones filled with drifting plankton, strange alien-like sea-life, and clusters of bizarre cocoons. When triggered the cocoons would burst open releasing their captive model and leaving them suspended in the dark aquatic world. The models rotated slowly in all directions, helping not only to enhance the illusion of weightlessness, but also presenting the outfits in detail from all directions. These interactive video sequences were also adapted for use in a supporting video banner campaign. Users were presented with more technical information relating to the outfits, and given the chance to buy individual items that made up the outfit, or to get the entire look.

The experience was executed down to the smallest of details, which included changing the behaviour of the user's mouse cursor so it felt as if it were being pulled through the water. With usability a major priority the experience was designed to ensure it was quick and easy to move between outfits. The experience also incorporated a simpler alternative navigation of the key outfits for low-bandwidth and the less time-rich shopper.

As new outfits were to be added weekly, the site was built around a flexible framework, enabling the site to be easily maintained. The Flash experience dynamically integrated with the rest of the online store, pulling in real-time product availability and seamlessly linking to the shopping cart and final sections of the purchasing process.

0 — Items remaining

x2 Unique visitors

4,300 Blog articles

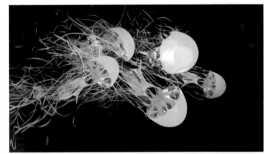

Style Lounge – Diesel Online Store

The Results

This was one of the most sophisticated interactive video experiences of its time created for the Web. It pushed the boundaries of online video production, bringing special effects and production levels previously seen only on the cinema and TV screen to the Web for the first time. It helped maintain Diesel's momentum as a forward-thinking and innovative brand.

The major goal of the "Style Lounge" was intended to provoke interest in Diesel.com during the launch of the online store. The "Style Lounge" provided an interesting PR angle for the launch, and increased the amount and quality of media coverage. Aside from being the focus of major press articles, it provoked many hundreds of positive blog posts. With the coinciding launch of both the "Style Lounge" and the main online store, there was no online sales history to compare with it, making the impact on sales hard to assess accurately. However, the "Style Lounge" was instrumental in fuelling online buzz that not only generated significantly increased site visits and subsequent sales, but, importantly, increased wide awareness of the e-commerce store, setting the foundations for long-term sales success.

The experience was extremely popular with visitors, who on average viewed five key outfits and spent seven minutes within the "Style Lounge", most of them then continuing to the main online store. The "Style Lounge" delivered a higher than average sales conversion, and all outfits which featured in the "Style Lounge" sold out.

The high-speed "Motion Photography" brought a new dimension to fashion photography, combining rich story-telling with exquisite product presentation. Not only were the outfits viewable from all angles, but the subtle movements of the garments helped to describe the nature of the fabrics. By exploiting the potential of interactive media to deliver a rich emotional experience, the user was brought as close to the product as possible without actually being able to touch it. The store would soon become Diesel's best performing outlet, outselling even Diesel's largest high-street flagship stores.

Volkswagen Autopilot

"One of the most original automotive
sites I have seen to date."
Rob Ford, FWA

The Brief

Volkswagen wanted an interactive campaign which would inform the public about its technical innovations. Ideally, it would bring visitors up to speed about Volkswagen's built-in technologies, while at the same time staying away from technical animations or long texts.

The Challenge

From a communication point of view the main challenge was to explain each innovation in a way that anybody could understand. We wanted to stay away from technical terms explaining *how* these complicated technologies work. Instead we wanted people to experience what these innovations actually *DO* for you.

We came up with a metaphor of using moving boxes, each box representing a car. In each box you could see the driver of that particular "car" and how they reacted to the situation they were in, or to the other "cars" around them.

The second challenge was to get the behaviour of the boxes right, and synching the box's movement and positioning with the driver's behaviour on video. Obviously, user experience had to be optimal, and this is always difficult when using interactive video.

Client
Volkswagen Pon's Automobile

Credits
Achtung!
www.achtung.nl
Volkswagen
www.volkswagen.nl

Awards
FWA, New York Festivals, Andy,
One Show, Webby

www.volkswagenautopilot.nl

The Solution

We translated each innovation to an easily recognisable icon. Each innovation had a scenario and the user had to choose the right innovation in the right scenario. This way, you could actually see what that specific innovation does in a real-life traffic situation. For example, everyone has trouble parking a car in a really tight space. By using Park Assist the car would actually park itself.

The icons were placed in a dashboard interface, so all you had to do was click on the corresponding icon. You'd get a simple explanation of what you just did and the Innovation you chose, thus adding an extra layer of information.

Getting the behaviour right was a matter of testing and tweaking: building the whole animation only to find out it didn't quite work and rebuilding the whole scenario.

The Results

The microsite was visited over 150,000 times in the first four weeks of the campaign. The banner campaign was the source of 10% of this traffic (0.55% CTR).

The campaign site generated a lot of attention at home but also abroad. It received Site of the Day from theFWA.com and was featured on many European advertising blogs.

Meanwhile, six other countries – which are co-ordinated from the German headquarters in Wolfsburg – want to adapt the site to their local needs. It was also chosen as the best interactive campaign of the Volkswagen AG, globally, by all the Volkswagen countries.

250,000 Site visits

7 Minutes average time on site

20,000 Google results

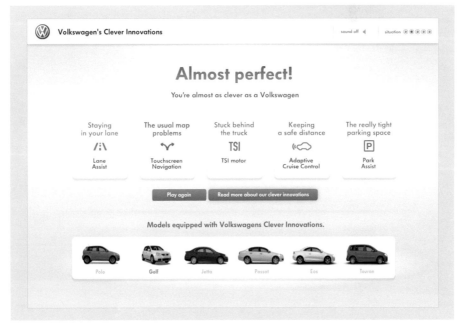

139

Nordstrom Backroom

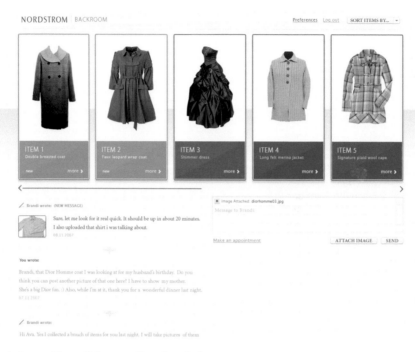

"Fantasy Interactive did a really nice job, and we appreciated the great support provided throughout the project."
Nordstrom Tech Team

Client
Nordstrom

Credits
Fi
www.f-i.com
Zeus Jones
www.zeusjones.com

www.f-i.com/work/nordstrom/
nordstroms-backroom

The Brief

Nordstrom Inc., one of the leading fashion retailers in the USA with over 173 stores located in 28 states, wanted an exclusive shopping experience for their most valued customers. Nordstrom desired an elegant Web experience allowing their sales staff and clients to gain access from anywhere, any time. Fi was approached by Zeus Jones to develop the prototype for this new shopping application for Nordstrom with a sharp focus on the precious impulse buy.

The Challenge

It was crucial that the application had a clean design and an intuitive interface. It should have the ability for sales personnel to communicate easily with the client, but also for the client to find information about any given "Backroom" product. The design had to inspire visitors to stay on the page as long as possible, and hopefully also find something beautiful to wear. Additionally, the entire nature of the application is for Personal Shoppers to upload photographs of special "Backroom" merchandise to the application quickly and easily.

The Solution
Fi created an invitation-only application service for exclusive customers to browse for fashion items selected personally for them by the Nordstrom salespeople. By smoothly integrating the merchandise database into two interfaces, one for the personal shopper and one for their clients with a "What you see is what you get" CMS interface, the salespeople could seamlessly manage their clients' selections. 3-D "cards" were used to present each item in a clear, concise way, inviting the customer to flip the card over for more information, just like a tag in the store. The interface was built for the wealthy shopper to quickly peruse their custom shopping list, while sipping a glass of wine and running their fingers along the numbers of their soon-to-be-charged plastic.

The Results
Nordstrom salespeople are able to find fashion picks for their clients more quickly and easily with the online interface. Thriving on real-time client interactions, managing their clients has become dramatically easier, and more lucrative. Sold over $30,000 within the first five minutes of launch, and converted their first purchase inside of 60 seconds.

10,000
U.S. dollars in monthly sales

9,500
Google results

60
Seconds after launch before first purchase

ITEM 3
Shimmer dress

DESCRIPTION
This shimmer dress is the
perfect piece for luxury lovers
ipsum dolor sit amet. Set ipsu
lorem ipsum dolor sit amet.

COLLECTION
Spring/Summer 2008

PIECE
Dress

WRAP IT UP
0 NO THANKS
$1299.00   return ›

ITEM 1
Double breasted coat
new   more ›

ITEM 2
Faux leopard wrap coat
new   more ›

ITEM 4
Long felt morning jacket
        more ›

ITEM 5
Signature plaid wool cape
        more ›

⟨   ⟩

✎ Brandi wrote: (NEW MESSAGE)

Sure, let me look for it real quick. It should be up in about 20 minutes.
I also uploaded that shirt i was talking about.
08.11.2007

☒ Image Attached diorhomme01.jpg
Message to Brandi

Make an appointment   ATTACH IMAGE   SEND

You wrote:

Brandi, that Dior Homme coat I was looking at for my husband's birthday. Do you
think you can post another picture of that one here? I have to show my mother.
She's a big Dior fan. :) Also, while I'm at it, thank you for a wonderful dinner last night.
07.11.2007

✎ Brandi wrote:

Hi Ava. Yes I collected a bunch of items for you last night. I will take pictures of them
first thing in the morning. Talk to you then. ps. I'm jelous of your new D&G bag!
07.11.2007

You wrote:

Brandi, that coat I was looking at for my husband's birthday
Do you think you can post another picture of that one here?
I have to show my mother. She's a big Dior fan. :) Also, while I'm at it,
thank you for a wonderful dinner last night.
07.11.2007

✎ Brandi wrote:

Hi Ava. Yes I collected a bunch of items for you last night. I will take pictures of them
first thing in the morning. Talk to you then. ps. I'm jelous of your new D&G bag!
07.11.2007

You wrote:

Brandi, that Dior Homme coat I was looking at for my husband's birthday. Do you
think you can post another picture of that one here? I have to show my mother.
She's a big Dior fan. :) Also, while I'm at it, thank you for a wonderful dinner last night.
07.11.2007

✎ Brandi wrote:

Hi Ava. Yes I collected a bunch of items for you last night. I will take pictures of them
first thing in the morning. Talk to you then. ps. I'm jelous of your new D&G bag!
07.11.2007

You wrote:

Brandi, that Dior Homme coat I was looking at for my husband's birthday. Do you
think you can post another picture of that one here? I have to show my mother.
She's a big Dior fan. :) Also, while I'm at it, thank you for a wonderful dinner last night.
07.11.2007

✎ Brandi wrote:

Hi Ava. Yes I collected a bunch of items for you last night. I will take pictures of them
first thing in the morning. Talk to you then. ps. I'm jelous of your new D&G bag!
07.11.2007

∧
∨

back up

CONTACT US   NORDSTROM PRIVACY

143

Canyon Bicycles

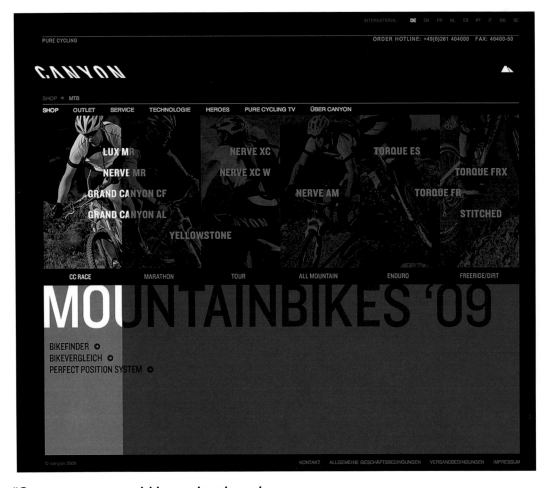

"Canyon never would have developed
the way it did without the website."
Roman Arnold, Founder & Owner of
Canyon Bicycles GmbH

Client
Canyon Bicycles GmbH

Credits
wysiwyg* software design
www.wysiwyg.de

Awards
Red Dot Award, iF Design Award

www.canyon.com

The Brief

For direct seller Canyon the online chop has become their major channel of distribution. Canyon seeks to supply fans and bicyclists online with all things bike, whilst ensuring topmost clarity, lucidity, and advisory skills throughout their website. All products and their different set-ups are presented lavishly and feature a zoom-in on the respective product pages. Canyon's Bike Finder allows easy selection of the desired model while the perfect positioning system provides correct size and seating configurations. Finally, Pure Cycling TV as well as Canyon Heroes add to the overall brand experience.

The Challenge

Provide the demanding target group of hobby cyclists who love technology with a complete set of information on Canyon bikes. The online shop should be supplemented with intelligent tools in order to reasonably help the consumer to select the right racing, mountain, or triathlon bike. Moreover, the increase of products over the past years demands a multi-level information architecture that still has to provide a maximum of clearness and usability. Navigation in combination with supporting tools should give the best possible answer to the question "which bike is best for me?"

The Solution

Canyon's website accomplishes the objectives with three all-new tools, which are unique in the segment of online bike shops: bike-finder, bike-comparator, and the perfect positioning system (www.canyon.com/_en/tools). They actually consult the target group by helping to find the ideal bike for every rider's conceivable needs, comparing bikes in detail as well as determining the ideal bike measurements. With the perfect positioning system, users can have an animated look at themselves on the bike of their choice. By selecting different models, handlebars, and seat settings, users can determine the perfect sitting position and the corresponding frame size. The clear navigation structure is another means to communicate the increasing portfolio quickly and easily.

The Results

Canyon.com manages to be a full-service bike website that has developed into a rather large (and really hard-selling, but still nice) platform, that offers not only unique consulting for buyers, but in addition delivers a large amount of further information and brand content. Now almost 80% of their business comes through their site. Business in total has grown by about 500% since the first evolution step from a "your logo here"-site to a real shop/showroom website.

80
Percent online distribution

500
Percent growth

30
Percent deficient orders reduced

21
Percent reduction of inquiries by phone

Sprint NOW Widget

"I love seeing that people are feeling comfortable
enough with data as a super abstract thing to start
playing with it and letting it be part of the creative
palette. There are incredible new possibilities."
Michael Lebowitz, Big Spaceship

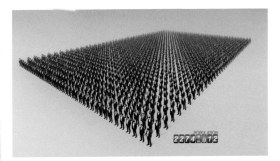

MOST POPULAR BREED : LABRADOR

The Brief

Demonstrate the immediacy of Sprint's data network and make it relevant to people's lives. We're fulfilling the original premise of mobile – of letting people connect wherever they are. What's changed are the ways in which we let people connect. Sprint provides the networks – 3G, voice, NDC, and 4G – that allow instantaneous connections. Our brand is about people, it's about what they feel when they make an instant connection. It's about living with a technology that can go everywhere. It's about always being connected, and connecting to the people, things, and stuff they love. It's about living right Now and celebrating the vast array of life that people can connect with thanks to Sprint's technology.

The Challenge

Telecom companies are starting to blur together these days. Most are touting offers and claims that change from day to day. Customers will jump from one provider to another, chasing the best deal of the moment or the lowest price because there's nothing else to latch on to. We saw an opportunity to make Sprint stand for something bigger. We wanted to give their network some humanity, so they could own that wonderful feeling people have when they get the data they want on their phones or laptops instantaneously.

Client
Sprint

Credits
Goodby, Silverstein & Partners
www.goodbysilverstein.com

http://now.sprint.com/nownetwork

Sprint NOW Widget

The Solution
Rather than talk about prices or calls dropped, we cut to the chase and renamed Sprint's network "the Now Network" and set to work linking Sprint with all things Now. Online, we designed the world's largest widget – a one-page snapshot of this very second. Live feeds and real-time facts flood the site, from babies being born to a live cam of Niagara Falls. Streaming data also filled ads across the Web, including an interactive Yahoo! takeover. Four television spots took visual cues from the site as well. The campaign launched with a :60 anthem that pulses with data, inundating viewers with all the things people are doing right now thanks to the Now Network, from blocking spam to Twittering to leaving phones in the backs of cabs.

The Results
Since the April 2009 launch, the campaign has been written up in over 100 publications and blogs, including The Wall Street Journal, the Los Angeles Times, engadget, and The New York Times. Beyond PR press, thousands of people have Twittered and blogged about the campaign.

In the first three weeks, the Now Network site racked up more than 1 million visits with an average of 15 interactions. Average time spent was 4 minutes – all on a one-page website. So far, Sprint has seen solid returns. Between April 6 and April 28, the online messaging delivered almost 340 million impressions, adding that brand exposure time was about 45 seconds per impression, close to double the wireless benchmark.

1
Million visits
(first 3 weeks)

340
Million impressions
for online messages

4
Minutes average
time on site

2
Times the wireless
benchmark for
brand exposure

COST OF LIVING NOW

NYC, NY
2.20

San
Francisco,
CA
1.73

Chicago,
IL
1.13

Topeka,
KS
0.90

CHECKING STOCKS
ON SPRINT PHONES

2704

Sprint

See more Now →

MOVIE TICKETS SOLD IN THE U.S.

3 2 3

POP NOW

Sprint

↻ Shuffle

See more Now →

SPRAY TANS SOLD IN THE U.S.

4 1 0 9

VIDEOS UPLOADED
ON SPRINT PHONES.

4 4 8

Sprint

↻ Shuffle

See more Now →

Promotional

Introduction by
Ajaz Ahmed, AKQA

03

Pro

motional

The best work isn't projected, it's shared
A third of the way through the 1979 cult-classic Quadrophenia (based on The Who's rock opera album of the same name) there is a scene where a condescending middle-aged, middle-class advertising executive sits with his two male colleagues in the agency's darkened smoky theatre. He barks orders at a young projectionist and his wayward mates in the back room to run a black and white television commercial. Depicting a good-looking, modern, aspirational couple enjoying a packet of cigarettes after a tough, typically rainy English day, this old-school cliché of an advertisement is intended to be more ironic comment than an illustration of the industry's best work and even if it wasn't for the repellent product it's trying to promote the ad is absolutely awful.

"Although some stuffy old-school agencies that are not in touch with their audience continue to produce identikit, predictable and patronizing advertising, the best work today isn't projected, it's shared."

While the agency executives seem rather pleased with their bland creation, set against the film's explosive backdrop of rebellious youth, working-for-the-weekend hedonism, illegal drugs, thrills, and headline chasing, none of the youths in the rear projection room show even a passing interest in the commercial. The advertising industry today couldn't be more different from the one portrayed in this film. Although some stuffy old-school agencies that are not in touch with their audience still exist and continue to produce identikit, predictable, and patronizing advertising, the best work today isn't projected, it's shared.

First. Or best?
Despite all the channels we have, the platforms we embrace and the devices we own, the best medium has been and always will be word of mouth. Any campaign that creates positive talkability will reward the advertiser. And today, more often than not, social media is where most of the conversations happen, capturing the mood of the moment. To understand where it's heading, let's reflect on how it has transformed marketing and advertising, and a brand's relationships with its consumers.

As with any great revolution, the social media one hasn't happened overnight. Many agencies were at first stumped by the emergence of digital, both how to use it and the value it added. In those early days, many organizations made the mistake of trying to apply old thinking to new media.

The result was the much derided online brochure because it didn't use the inherent power of interactivity. If that mindset had prevailed, it's questionable whether we would have ever seen the creation of social networks, sophisticated online services or applications purpose-built for mobile phones. The award-winning delights now created by agencies prove that it's not necessarily who is first to market, but who is best.

Simplicity is the ultimate sophistication
By its very definition, social media requires a new mindset to engage effectively with consumers. Print and broadcast advertising is one-way – it's static and inert, and the call to action lies with the consumer to decide whether the product or service is desirable enough and the advert is compelling enough to make the effort and investment to purchase. Social media offers a whole new level of flexibility, interaction, and engagement. It is that ability to create a compelling experience that has captivated brands and consumers alike.

"The key word is 'experience' – to engage fully with a brand, consumers today expect a healthy new dialogue that enables them to converse easily with an organization."

The key word is "experience" – to engage fully with a brand, consumers today expect a healthy new dialogue that enables them to converse easily with an organization, and the ecosystem that supports it. Social media lends itself to this behavior, brands to this opportunity, and consumers to this experience. But brands should be wary of blitzing their consumers with technology just for the sake of it – if consumers have to hack their way through unnecessary or complicated features that deter them from understanding the key message, benefit, the premise, or if there's a barrier to the dialogue, then they will switch off as that's the easiest option available.

The best advertising isn't advertising
The sheer vastness of choices available and the accessibility of them to just about everyone means that we are all living more hectic personal and professional lives giving rise to more noise and clutter clamoring for our attention. Greater mobility and access to online services is transforming the way we think about work, rest and play.

Against that, a far smarter approach for a brand to engage with a consumer is to offer services that make life easier. With this approach, social media creates a model where advertising isn't advertising any more. It takes it to a much more sophisticated level, where the consumer gains access to a useful, beneficial, enjoyable service which fulfils a need rather than conventional brand-name blasting.

Tuning in to "channel me"

Perhaps the next challenge for marketers is how to effectively target consumers in the era of "channel me". Thanks to social media, it has never been easier for individuals to affirm their identity, share their thoughts, interests, and concerns with their friends, family, or anyone else paying attention. Performing on their customized online stage, the consumer has now become their own brand, and one that commands an audience of its own. Photographs, stories, updates, interests, events, playlists, and hobbies are some of the constituent parts that create this brand "me" with its own campaign to influence friends and win new ones. And since the consumer is busy with the challenge of building and promoting their own brand, it makes it all the more difficult for organizations to increase their connection, ensure their relevance, and win attention for the products that they own.

> **"As the examples in this chapter illustrate, the best way to create the future is to make your work live fully in the present."**

Keeping on track

As the examples in this chapter illustrate, the best way to create the future is to make your work live fully in the present. Predicting the future is of course not an exact science but one thing is for sure: the advertising executives pictured in Quadrophenia, and the industry that they represent, are thankfully things of the past.

Ajaz Ahmed
AKQA

Bio.
Ajaz Ahmed
AKQA

Ajaz Ahmed is the chairman of AKQA. Ajaz co-founded AKQA and works with clients to develop new product ideas, identify trends and opportunities.

AKQA employs around 850 people. A recognized pioneer and innovator, AKQA has helped create some of the world's most influential and iconic work.

One of the world's most-awarded agencies, AKQA has been named Agency of the Year twelve times and is the only agency to hold the title Agency of the Year on both sides of the Atlantic at the same time, three years running. It was most recently named Advertising Agency of the Year by *Creative Review* magazine.
–
www.akqa.com

"The best medium has been, and always will be word of mouth"

AKQA Christmas Card 2008

"Ideas company AKQA has created
one of the coolest Christmas
cards I've ever seen..."
Gizmodo

The Brief
Wish all our friends and clients a Happy Christmas in an innovative and entertaining way. It sounds easy, but Christmas is a time when every agency is working to exactly the same brief.

The Challenge
2007's effort was always going to take some beating. Picture the scene – two gerbils, named "Cheese" and "Biscuits", sat in a custom-made "stage" of glass. Before them, a video camera streaming video live to the Web. Behind them, a huge neon sign wishing everybody "Happy Christmas from AKQA". Inside their domain was a specially adapted hamster wheel. The wheel was wired up to the neon sign and every time one of our little friends took to their wheel, the sign would illuminate. The world's first gerbil-powered-digital-neon-festive-agency-greeting was born. Needless to say, it caused a vast amount of stir in the press and gained unprecedented industry interest, as well as accolades. We had struck originality square on. But that was last year. This time, we had to go one better.

Client
AKQA

Credits
AKQA
www.akqa.com
Bikini
www.bikinifilms.co.uk
AKQA Film
www.akqa.com

Awards
Creative Circle Awards, Creative Review Annual, One Show, The Independent

http://akqa.com/happychristmas

AKQA Christmas Card 2008

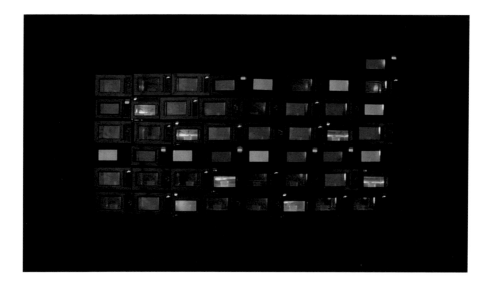

The Solution

Rodents were out. Neon too. After the incident with the gnawed wiring and the subsequent settlement with Cheese and Biscuits' agent, we plumped for simplicity and tradition.

The phone rang at just the right moment. Timing is everything. An anonymous friend, a delivery driver by trade, had a job lot of catering-quality microwaves on his hands and wondered if we were interested. What would we do with 50 industrial microwaves?! Ping! Calls were made. Friends roped. Studio booked and 49 microwaves were stacked, powered up and painstakingly choreographed to create a completely new rendition of Jingle Bells.

The idea was so simple that it didn't rely on language, location, bandwidth, or gerbils. It didn't require much effort on the recipient's part, didn't hog the bandwidth, and didn't cause entire workforces to grind to a halt. It simply raised a smile and wished every viewer a Happy Christmas from AKQA.

The Results

The film had racked up over one million views by Christmas Day and is totalling over two million now. It has received acclaim and attention from TV networks, radio shows, clients, friends, family, bloggers, environmentalists, electrical retailers, and health and safety officials the world over.

AKQA's Christmas message appeared on the MSN homepage, was the No. 1 featured video on YouTube UK, France, Germany, and Japan. It was posted by American music artist Kanye West as his only blog message on Christmas Day, and even Jay Leno asked if we could pop over to the US and create the piece on the Tonight Show. As well as a blog list that reads like a telephone directory, the film was featured in Wired, The Guardian, Campaign, Advertising Age, Creative Review, Boards, Shots, Gizmodo, The Independent, Agency Spy, and Current TV.

 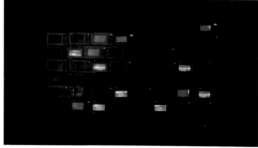

#1
YouTube video in UK,
France, Germany, and Japan

2
Million views

Elf Yourself

"Forget the Subservient Chicken
and Whopper Freakout. When
it comes to digital campaigns,
Office Max's Elf Yourself has left
them all in the dust"
Advertising Age

The Brief

It is nearly impossible for a retail client to stand out using traditional marketing and a modest budget in the infamous fourth quarter. In 2006, Office Max and Toy approached EVB with an unconventional proposal. They were going to take their entire Q4 budget and create a series of viral marketing sites. The site should have something to do with uploading your face on to a dancing elf. After a Craig's List casting call, a trip to a costume store, and a green-screen shoot in an empty part of EVB's space, Elf Yourself was born.

The Challenge

Office Max is a generic office-supply store, hardly the first destination consumers consider for their holiday shopping, especially against an ever-increasing backdrop of intense retail competition during that time of year. It was no easy task, but EVB & Toy decided it was time to change that. Office Max truly was a great choice for selecting gifts. In fact, their prices were on a par with not better than their more top-of-mind "holiday" competition.

Client
Office Max

Credits
Evolution Bureau (EVB)
http://evb.com
Toy
www.toyny.com

Awards
FWA, Ad-Tech, SXSW, One Show Interactive

http://elf.evb-archive.com

The Solution

Our idea was simple… everyone loves to send greetings cards during the holidays. But it was our interactive high-tech twist on this tradition that worked to give consumers a new way to connect with loved ones and became an overnight "e-phenomenon". During the holidays, millions of bored office workers sit around surfing the Web social-networking networking sites and uploading audio or video. We tapped into this desire for self-expression and built a short, snack-like tidbit of online humor that fit well into a multi-tasking workday.

The campaign included a series of funny e-cards that could be customized by uploading people's faces on to the bodies of holiday elves. It let participants feature their friends and family members as cheerful dancing elves along with a toll-free number that let people customize an audio greeting. Users could then forward on to loved ones and post links on their blogs, personal websites, and social-networking profiles. In 30 short days we created a viral sensation… one that has yet to be beaten by any other digital advertiser.

GREAT GIFTS NOW AT **OfficeMax**   TERMS OF USE   PRIVACY POLICY   FEEDBACK

Provided by OfficeMax® under license from FlaFusion LLC to U.S. Patent Nos. 6.361.265 and 5.623.587

The Results

The results far and away exceeded everyone's expectations. Nearly one in ten Americans "elfed themselves" and it quickly became the 55th most popular website in the world. ElfYourself.com had over 193 million visits that included the "elfamorphosis" of over 123 million people creating viral value for Office Max. 60 elves were created per second at its peak. That's more than the population of California, Australia, and France, combined.

Site visitors spent an average of seven minutes on the site itself that totaled 2.5 thousand years of cumulative time interacting with the site and the brand. Mass PR generated by mainstream media including the early morning news shows such as Good Morning America, CNN American Morning, ABC World News, TNT Sportscast, Fox News, TBS and Rosie O'Donnell's Blog, and The TODAY Show, helped catapult adoption of this site as the quintessential holiday e-card.

In addition, a brand study conducted by Office Max found that nearly half of consumers asked attributed the Elf Yourself campaign to the Office Max brand. And more than one-third of those visiting Elf Yourself claimed the site influenced their decision to shop at Office Max. Linking the site to officemax.com also drove referral traffic that resulted in a 190% lift over normal traffic levels. And, the Elf has now become Office Max's holiday "icon" and is featured in-store and in direct mail efforts and is a character they can truly own.

225 Million site visits

60 Peak Elves created per second

569,000 Results on Google

Who is Fermin? – One Million Clicks

"One Million Clicks project is a
fun experience that challenges
the user's abilities."
Miguel Calderon, GrupoW

Client
Unilever, Rexona

Credits
GrupoW
www.grupow.com

Awards
FWA, Webby, New York Festivals,
Flash in the Can, Wave, Circulo
de Oro, El Sol, FIAP, Ojo de
Iberoamerica, Cannes

www.grupowprojects.com

The Brief

Rexona released in 2007 its new product, Rexona Power, whose main characteristic was that it contained one million molecules for under-arm protection. One Million Clicks campaign was a challenge because we needed to collect 1,000,000 clicks from users so we could "Save Fermin" and release the second stage of the project.

Fortunately for us, the strategy worked and the campaign could be developed as it was intended from the beginning. Who the #!%$ is Fermin, the hotsite of the campaign, showed the exact moment when all the obstacles chase Fermin in a frozen second… after all this, the product is shown as a deodorant, but we thought that if we presented it in a fun way through an interactive story to its consumers, it would be much more interesting for the users and the brand.

The Challenge

The main target is the so-called "Rexona man" segment, people between 25 and 35 who are aware about their own personal hygiene and want to get on with what they do without worrying about sweat stains, so Rexona Power provides them with a safe solution. The challenge was to get over to the user how the product contains over one million molecules. For this, we needed a clever idea.

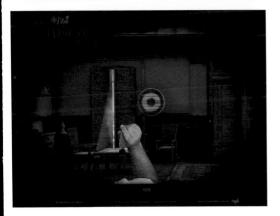

The Solution

First, a fake organization ran an extensive national crusade to raise one million clicks to save Fermin. At its website, visitors were asked to donate a click to save the spirit of "living life to its fullest, and never to relinquish it"; after their contribution, donors could download an authenticity certificate for their click, with a unique and non-repeating number.

At this stage, nothing was revealed about the so-called Fermin nor did the site mention the brand or the product. During the one-month intense campaign, through various means and activities throughout the streets of Mexico, the audience got deeply engaged in what would later become a media phenomenon. Hundreds of forums in various countries were talking about Fermin, making the campaign into a marketing and advertising case study for several universities.

The Results

In just a few weeks, two million users had donated five-hundred thousand clicks. And then the strategy changed: the website became a countdown warning, urging users to complete the click donations in just one week. The support video, published on YouTube, made it to the Top Ten in the week it was launched.

Finally, when the goal was reached, the "Who is Fermin?" experience went live, answering the question created by the fake organization. On this site, the user had to deal with various perils, which, when solved, would compel them to realize that they too own the Fermin spirit.

With media coverage both online and offline, the campaign was a huge success in the country, exceeding somehow the limits of the virtual world in which it was born.

4.5 Million hits

1 Million clicks recorded

20,000 Certificates issued

45,000 YouTube views

100,000 Donations to Mexico City streets

White Gold

"I sat on their website for two hours playing the little games and learning trivia about a band that isn't really real. Then I went to YouTube to watch 'Tame the White Tiger' again. The line 'sharing a cold glass with the white monkey!' really gets me every time; I laugh so hard. I've changed my status in Facebook to lyrics from some of the songs."
Kyle P, age 16, Fremont, CA

Client
The California Milk Processor Board

Credits
Goodby, Silverstein & Partners
www.goodbysilverstein.com
Odopod
www.odopod.com

Awards
FWA, Effie, Festival of Media, Mediaweek, FiTC, New York Festivals, One Show, Clios, Cannes, LIA

www.whitegoldiswhitegold.com

WHITE GOLD

The Brief

When kids become teenagers, milk falls off their radar screens. They're away from home more and gravitating toward drinks with cool images that purport to offer various benefits: vitamin waters, iced teas, energy drinks, sports drinks. The truth is that milk does more than all those drinks to make a teen look and feel good. But milk is the boring old guy in the corner. Teens just don't think about milk.

Our brief was to connect with California teens and transform milk from something they see as uninteresting and inherently uncool, into something worth drinking more of. The opportunity was to use milk's benefits for hair, nails, teeth, and muscles to position milk as a vanity drink. And to let the message play out in teens' natural habitat: online.

The Challenge

The creative challenge was threefold:
- We had to come up with a creative device that could deliver the rational milk benefit information in a highly entertaining package.
- We wanted to make milk cool, but since milk isn't, we couldn't come at this straight on. The creative device had to be something that didn't try too hard to make milk cool. It had to not take itself too seriously. It had to be fun and likable.
- And last, since teens live much of their waking life in a digital world, we wanted to come up with a creative idea that we could take to where they are: social-networking sites, video sites, music sites.

The Solution

The answer: a fictional rock band. White Gold embodies – and sings about – all the benefits of milk. They are over-the-top and fun, in the spirit of Will Ferrell, Austin Powers, and Zoolander, reflecting the random and weird humor that teens gravitate toward.

We used the "what would a real band do?" filter to determine the content (a five-song EP, "The Best I Can Give is 2%," and three full-length music videos) and how it would live online, which included:

- Band profile pages on MySpace and Facebook
- Videos on YouTube
- A slick band website (like what the record label would put out)
- Songs on iTunes, Pandora, and Last.fm
- A Guitar Hero-meets-Simon Says Facebook application called "Thrashteurizer"

We went to where teens live, and gave them things worth passing on to their friends.

The Results

In less than a year, White Gold has entered California teen pop culture.

Tracking studies found that 42% of California teens who engaged with White Gold someplace online have talked to a friend about it. The percentage of teens who said they wouldn't drink milk in front of their friends dropped 23%. And teens' linkage of milk to key benefits like strong hair, nails, muscles, and teeth was up 22%.

Last, in extensive qualitative research, we've seen that White Gold has been able to do something we never thought possible: get "milk" and "cool" and "hip" used in the same sentence.

638,368 Visits

2:26 Minutes average
time on site

1.4 Million YouTube
views

Prince of Persia

"One of the best trailers ever."
User comment, gametrailers.com

The Brief

For Christmas 2008, Ubisoft's ambition was to make the first episode of the new Prince of Persia trilogy the #1 action-adventure gaming blockbuster. This episode is a new beginning with a new storyline, new character, and most importantly it has a brand new visual identity. The goal was to build excitement and anticipation among the fans of the series, attract the more mainstream gamers, and generate buzz and brand awareness through the sheer quality of the production. The keywords for communication were epic, graceful, deep, fascinating, and thoughtful.

The Challenge

The online marketing team asked Soleil Noir to create an experience that would convey the epic scale of the game that celebrates the art of movement in its acrobatic and fighting dimensions. Communicating this new sensation to the viewer was our main challenge. As it's a new beginning for Prince of Persia we had to create something different focusing on the artworks and story rather than the gameplay. It was all about keeping the efficiency of an experience site without needing much interactivity.

CEUX QUI ONT TENTÉ DE RÉSISTER ONT SUCCOMBÉ, ANÉANTIS PAR LES REDOUTABLES LÉGIONS D'AHRIMAN.

POUR SURVEILLER SA PRISON ÉTERNELLE, UNE TRIBU DE GUERRIERS A ÉTÉ CHOISIE. ELLE DEVAIT S'ASSURER QUE LES ALLIÉS DE L'OMBRE NE PUISSENT JAMAIS LIBÉRER LE DIEU DES TÉNÈBRES.

Client
Ubisoft EMEA

Credits
Soleil Noir
www.soleilnoir.net

Awards
FWA Theater, GameTrailers.com

www.princeofpersiagame.com/

The Solution
We've decided not to have the user interacting with the experience but to prepare their senses to be blasted with emotion. To achieve this a detailed storyboard highlighting the prequel of the story was produced by the agency. From there, voiceover text was written and recorded, sound designed, and 2-D artworks were brought to life. It gave us the enjoyment of creating something new rather than manipulating game footage and the result is a deep and immersive video introduction for the official website.

The Results
The result was a lot more than expected. From a website introduction we moved to a story trailer with a strong viral dimension. The video was captured and spread all over the Web with great comments attached. With a peak of over 300,000 unique visitors in the first week we exceeded our expectations.

   This production is for Ubisoft a great benchmark in terms of viral video and for Soleil Noir an achievement in art direction and motion design.

2 Million unique visitors

190,000 Video views

9.4 Video rating

325,000 Registrations

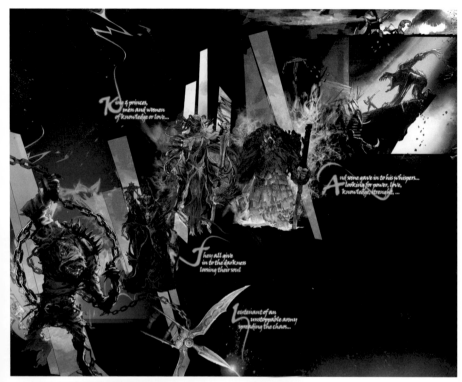

King & princes,
men and women
of knowledge or love...

And some gave in to his whispers...
looking for power, love,
knowledge, strenght, ...

They all give
in to the darkness
loosing their soul

Lieutenant of an
unstoppable army
spreading the chaos...

Launchball

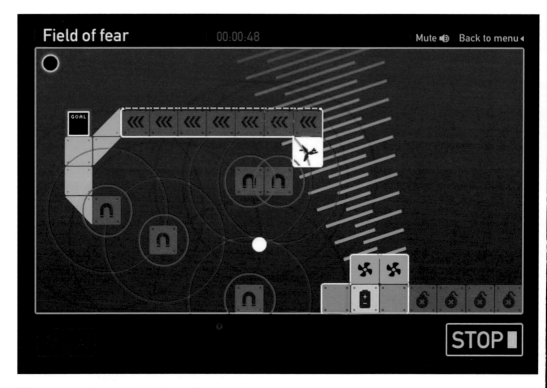

"It's very well executed, really smart, and merges playability with great information about physics. It's really a perfect campaign and it deserves the Gold."
Brice Le Blévennec, Eurobest Interactive Jury

Client
The Science Museum, London

Credits
Preloaded
www.preloaded.com

Awards
FWA, Eurobest, SXSW, Flash in the Can, Museums and the web, D&AD, Creative Review Annual

www.preload.us/launchball

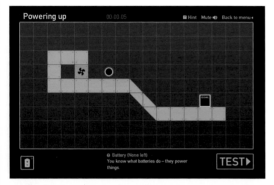

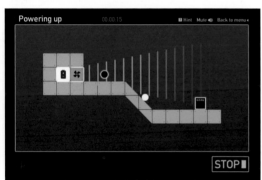

The Brief

The Science Museum wanted to develop an educational game to promote the opening of their revamped Launchpad Gallery. They wanted it to be available not only online, but also in kiosk form for use within the gallery itself, and for the game to feature a social and user-generated aspect to it. Most importantly, the game needed to teach children between the ages of eight and fourteen about the basic scientific principles of physics in an engaging manner. Careful consideration of how to include key physics-related phenomena and how to tie these all together in a cohesive experience was critical.

The Challenge

Balancing the educational remit with the playfulness of a game was always going to be a challenge. Each block had to have a specific set of physical properties that defined how it affects the blocks around it and any balls in play. These needed to include surface friction and bounce, conductivity of heat and electricity, and responses to those energies as well as wind, water, and light. Some also had to have a direct attractive/repulsive effect on a ball. The whole game would be driven by the interplay and balance of these forces and effects. The game would drip feed help and instructions to the player whilst educational "factoids" are delivered contextually after each level is completed. Blocks needed to be colour-coded in themes; for instance, pink for physical, white for electric, and green for neutral.

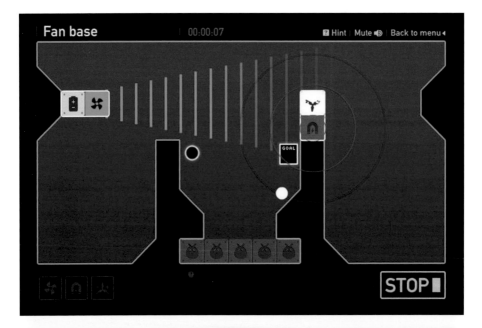

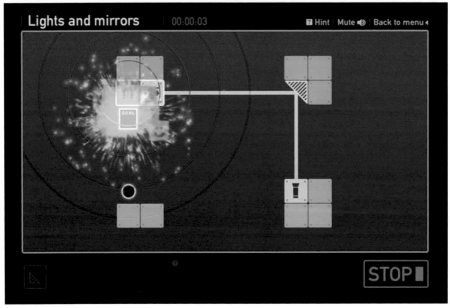

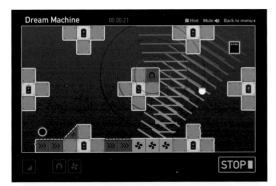

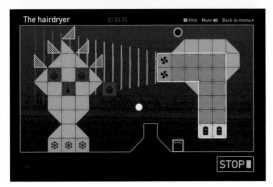

The Solution

In its simplest form Launchball is a level-based game with one objective: to get a ball to a goal in order to complete each stage. The player must use and master a set of blocks with physics-related properties in order to do this. The level structure and focus on the ball keeps the sense of a game whilst the blocks provide the educational touch-points across the 36 levels available.

In addition to this, a level-designer allows users to create their own levels and share them with friends, the best of which are featured on the Science Museum site. A competition to encourage people to create their most fiendish level designs has resulted in visitors building and sharing over 100,000 levels.

The Results

Within days of launching, the game was Digg'd over a thousand times, spreading the link quickly through the Internet; this huge level of word-of-mouth interest means a Google search for Launchball currently returns 84,000 results specific to the game. With Launchball being blogged about globally, game walkthroughs have quickly appeared across the Web, including several comprehensive YouTube tutorials by passionate fans. The game has attracted over 12 million visits, and over four million unique visitors.

12 Million visits

4 Million unique users

150,000 Registrations

1,082 Diggs in 24 hours

110,000 User-generated levels created

Eminem

"Can we make the text bigger,
Paul (Eminem's manager) has
problems reading."
Client

The Brief

Martin: The brief on this from what I remember was: "Can you make Eminem's site?", I don't think they gave us any starting point or direction. Which was rather pleasant because usually a client will hire us, then barge into the middle of the circle and bust some horrendous moves while WEFAIL grin through gritted teeth and clap along.

Jordan: I remember Marshall saying something about making the shit dope. And I said: "So you want the dope shit?" And he said: "No I want the shit dope." This went back and forth for a while and I just gave up. I think he was eating painkillers like tic-tacs.

The Challenge

Martin: It was to promote Eminem's new Greatest Hits album, I think. Yes, I have just Googled it, Curtain Call. I'm pretty sure no one had heard of Eminem before WEFAIL threw him into the limelight. He's a very lucky boy.

Jordan: You can't really win this one. He's already completely famous. You can't really lose either. The only highlight is wowing friends and family when they ask you what you're working on. And by highlight I mean it's a nice change from trying to explain who the f#+k Bob Schneider is for the thousandth time.

Client
Aftermath Records

Credits
WEFAIL
www.wefail.com

Awards
FWA, SXSW

http://wefail.com/eminem/

The Results

Martin: The result was that we had to argue and bicker to win petty little battles with the client. The client being a giant gaggle of faceless people that would email and ask for us to make the text bigger, A LOT BIGGER. Like full-screen size bigger, so that Eminem's cranky old manager, Paul, could read it. We never actually got to deal with Eminem directly, there were far too many lawyers to get through.

Jordan: Well my result was getting drunk and calling everyone at Interscope "c#+%s" in an email I cc'd to all the people we were working for. Imagine Martin waking up to that thread of emails in jolly England! It sounds kind of dashing but it was completely accidental... I was totally off my head on simple beer. I remember jellyfish man (as we'd come to call our contact, who NEVER stood up for us or the project) emailing directly back: "heeey, you don't have to call us all c#+%s." And I was like "Oooops, I think I've just emailed all of them and called them all c#+%s." Funny thing though is that it did help get their ass in gear and finally release the site.

Martin: Hahahaha, I'd forgotten about that. Ahhhh, our golden years.

The Solution

Martin: We decided to show his life, from obscurity on a trailer park to him dying and the Record Label squeezing every last ounce of money out of his rotting bones. For what it's worth we got his future pretty bloody accurate. He died, didn't he?

Jordan: Yeah, I really can't believe we got away with showing the record executives for the pigs they are. It reminds me of "The Money-Go-Round" by The Kinks: "Do they all deserve money from a song that they've never heard?" There's no way any of those pigs ever bothered to look at his website while it was up.

100 Terabytes of bandwidth on launch

1 Million Diggs

Ford Truck F150

"We needed to stay true to the Built Ford Tough brand and show the F-150 put a smack down on the competition. Partnering up with RED, based on their impactful UFC portfolio, was the obvious choice."
Stuart O'Neil, Group Creative Director, Digital, Wunderman – Team Detroit

The Brief

On the heels of a worldwide oil shortage that punished sales of large trucks and SUVs, Ford Motor Company and Wunderman Team Detroit needed to promote the debut of their All-New '09 F-150 as effectively as possible. They needed a website that would tell their story more powerfully than ever while still preserving integration with their extensive national campaign. The site would need to talk about the F-150's many advancements, about its rich multi-decade history, and about the look and feel of the new models. The site would need to remind visitors that the F-150 is America's best-selling full-size pick-up truck but more importantly, the site needed to remind America why.

The Challenge

For the last 31 years Ford has produced America's best-selling truck. However, the skyrocketing gas prices of 2008 coupled with the flagging US economy caused a shift in automotive sales trends. Light-duty pick-up sales were down 17% through April 2008 with an increasing number of truck owners looking to purchase cars, CUVs , and hybrids. The new F-150 campaign needed to embrace, but also aim beyond the traditional Ford target audience of "Joe Construction" and "DIY-Go-to-Guy", to include a new "Tough and Innovative" group concerned about fuel efficiency. To find that new crowd, the campaign would emphasize fuel efficiency in addition to several new advanced features of the new F-150.

Client
Ford

Credits
Wunderman – Team Detroit
www.teamdetroit.com
RED Interactive Agency
www.ff0000.com

Awards
FWA

www.fordvehicles.com/2009f150/

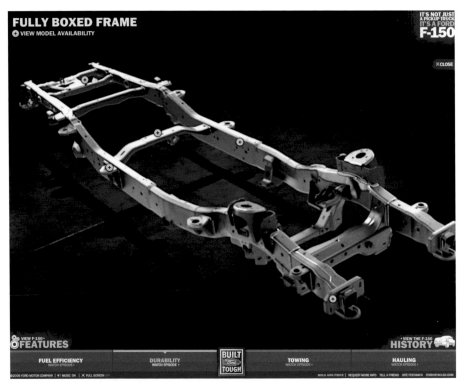

1.1
Million site visits

29
Percent increase in "build and price"

81
Percent video completion rate

The Solution

To effectively tell the F-150 story, four full-screen video episodes were produced featuring actor/personality Mike Rowe testing the F-150 against the competition. During each episode (Durability, Towing, Hauling, and Fuel Efficiency) users can compare the F-150 to competing trucks using a side-by-side interactive "Compare Cam." Following each of the four main video episodes, interactive hotspots appear over the truck to show mini-videos of key advancements with authentic demonstrations. An "Advancements Quick Nav" was also created to view the wide range of innovative new features available on the truck. Finally, the "History of Tough" was developed in the form of an interactive historical timeline, showing the development of the F-150 over the last century and featuring multiple vintage Ford ads and commercials.

The Results

The combination of demonstrating the F-150's advances, recounting its long history, and reminding site visitors that it is the best-selling truck in its class proved to be powerful. Watching the F-150's superiority on the "Compare Cam" was extremely effective as well. At its highest point, the site videos saw an average completion rate of 81%. The truck's rebounding sales may be the clearest indication of the site's success. The F-Series outsold its nearest truck rival by more than 50,000, and the F-150 is once again America's best-selling vehicle of any type.

189

Death in Sakkara

"Original, engaging, high-quality presentation.
Informative and enlightening – easily as good as
commercial games. Great fun all round. Brilliant!"
BBCi Online Survey

Client
BBC, Factual & Learning

Credits
Preloaded
www.preloaded.com

Awards
FWA, New Media, Flash Forward,
D&AD, Creative Review

www.deathinsakkara.com

The Brief
The BBC produced a four-part TV drama about the discovery of tombs and relics of ancient Egypt in the 1920s, recreating events surrounding the exciting archaeological finds of the time. For the online counterpart the main stipulation was that everything was based in historical fact, whilst also being entertaining and immersive, bringing the story of discovering ancient Egypt to life.

The Challenge
It was vital that we developed an engaging and entertaining experience which would really hook the incredibly wide player demographic. Getting the balance of gameplay and linear storytelling was an important part of the process, as was ensuring that we retained the "soft" learning elements which were a key part of the brief. Devising a mechanic which facilitated all of these issues was a major creative challenge, as was the process of testing and ensuring a great user experience.

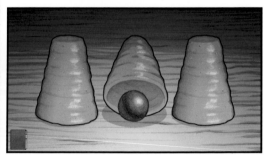

The Solution

Rather than emulating the show itself, an interactive narrative was developed that was capable of working both as a stand-alone experience and as value-added content for the television series, giving the site longevity beyond the broadcast dates. "Death in Sakkara" tells the story of a journalist drawn into intrigue and danger as he searches for a missing friend. Presented in the style of a pulp-fiction comic-book of the era it is steeped in a dark "Indiana Jones" tone. Games and puzzles along the way push the player through a story packed full of surprises and plot twists, all developed and scripted in conjunction with the BBC Factual and Learning team and Egyptology experts.

Importantly the game educates and informs throughout. An interactive journal is filled with Charles' thoughts and observations as the player progresses, quickly becoming a compendium of Egyptology, which can be checked at any time. It yields vital clues critical to success, as well as background information on items and events encountered along the way. Using this and their guile the player must see the quest through to its grisly conclusion.

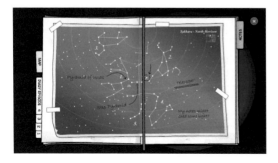

250,000

Users in first two months

75,000

Registrations in the first 2 months

42

Percent of users under 26

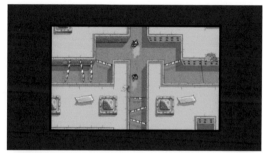

The Results

A huge number of individuals signed up to play "Death in Sakkara" in the first two months, placing it among the BBC's most successful registration-based sites almost immediately. Over a quarter of a million people played as unregistered guests in the first month, with 60% of players recommending the game to friends. A survey of users revealed that more than half were women and 42% were under 26 years old, both groups not traditionally BBC History audiences, whilst not alienating older audiences. 84% of players said that they learned something about Egyptology through playing "Death in Sakkara", and three quarters of those went on to explore other content on the BBC History site as a result.

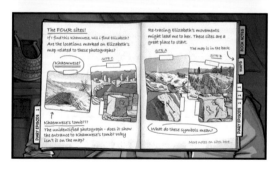

Doritos the Quest

"Any site that can engage a user for over ten minutes, on average, is worthy of huge praise."
Rob Ford, FWA

Client
Frito-Lay

Credits
The Marketing Arm
www.daviebrown.com
RED Interactive Agency
www.ff0000.com

Awards
FWA, Webby

www.doritosthequest.com

The Brief

Frito-Lay wanted to promote the launch of a new mystery flavor of Doritos. The goal was to engage consumers with an online game that featured a series of Flash-based puzzles and experiences that revolved around the iconic triangle shape. The game unfolded over the course of four phased launches, with new puzzles being released at each launch. Players competed against the ticking clock and each other as the challenges become increasingly difficult to overcome. In the end, the top three players were invited to compete in a real-world "Fear Factor" type event for a grand prize of $100,000.

The Challenge

The Quest campaign presented exciting challenges, specifically with regard to the concepting and creation of the various puzzles. The goal was to create over 15 unique puzzles that become increasingly more difficult as players progressed through the experience. The design team was also tasked with integrating the ever-present triangle symbol into each puzzle design, thereby reinforcing the brand and maintaining a common thread throughout every aspect of the site. Moreover, unlike most campaigns where the goal is to continue building a targeted user base, the goal of The Quest was to start out with a large audience and narrow it down to a final few. The Quest was not for everyone. Only the wittiest made it to the end.

The Solution

RED created a game that wove various puzzles into a grander online experience. Puzzles were organized into "chapters" and ranged in complexity from simple memory sequences to difficult logic puzzles. No specific instructions were provided, so users had to be clever and deduce the best way to solve each puzzle. The puzzles had to be solved in succession, with certain key puzzles revealing mysterious artifacts that would later serve as clues or play other integral roles in the experience. Successful players had to stay sharp, as The Quest could not be tamed without developing skills like deciphering an alphabet that was created specifically for this game. As a player's skills grew, so did their chances of becoming one of the three people to compete for the $100,000 grand prize.

The Results

Over 650,000 people began playing the game and only a few thousand made it to the end. It was a war of attrition and most people withered under the pressure. For the final puzzle, thousands of answers were submitted within the initial hours of the puzzle being released, but the first correct answer was not submitted until approximately eight hours later. The final puzzle was so challenging that most of the players eventually yielded to exhaustion and submitted a random guess. Yet a second correct answer came in after around 11 hours, and the third was finally logged in at around the 12-hour mark. The players who submitted these three answers were the ones who were given the opportunity to compete for the grand prize.

70,000
Registered users

660,000
Unique visitors

10:48
Minutes average time on site

CDX

"Exceptional attention to detail and
high production values set this effort
apart from other adventures... another
remarkable production from Preloaded."
Jay Bibby, jayisgames.com

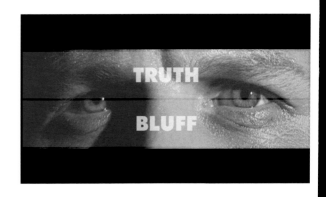

The Brief

The brief was to create an interactive film with immersive gaming elements to play alongside a six-part television show about Ancient Rome. Core to the proposition was to include educational content in a non-traditional way, being discreetly informative. There was also a desire to push the boundaries of previous interactive narrative work undertaken for the History department, namely, the award-winning site "Death in Sakkara" Preloaded had delivered previously.

The Challenge

The story-line of the game takes the form of a dark contemporary thriller set in the background of the series broadcast on television. The central narrative premise – a prop man working on the show becomes embroiled in intrigue and dark happenings – takes the story beyond the broadcast. We developed the plot in conjunction with the BBC, their scriptwriter, and a Roman History consultant, and together we ensured that dramatic purpose and historical accuracy were at the centre of the experience.

 is referenced above; text in right margin: 03 Promotional

Client
BBC, Factual & Learning

Credits
Preloaded
www.preloaded.com

Awards
FWA, Cannes Lions,
Royal Television Society, Flash
Forward, YDAwards, D&AD

http://cdx-thegame.com

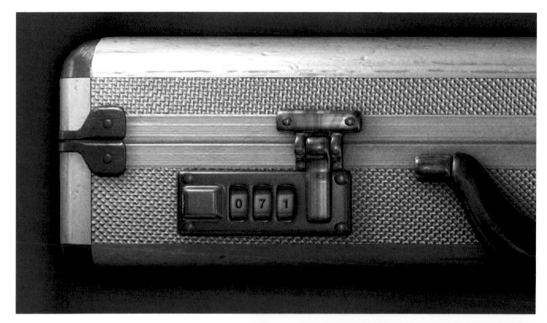

The Solution

The project was the first in which the BBC combined online and interactive television budgets, enabling us to develop elements from the programme within the online experience, and vice versa. For example, the game's central character, Adam Foster, appears in the show's closing credits as the prop man, to add that extra link between the two and a layer of credibility. We worked in 3-D to plan and model the environments the live action was to be keyed into. The main challenge was combining the video footage with the CGI elements seamlessly, ensuring all angles matched and the filmic quality was retained. Hundreds of clips of video offer the player a raft of routes through, and a number of possible resolutions to the story depending on the choices made during their game. This created a level of depth not previously achieved online.

The Results

CDX was rolled out in four phases, sequentially unlocked as instalments of the six-part television programme went to air. The game was then released to a global audience with the support of Adobe, who sponsored the international version, seeing it as a great example of what could be achieved with their creative and interactive tools. To date the experience has attracted 1.2 million unique visitors.

1.2
Million unique users

180
Flash video files

5,000
Hours development time

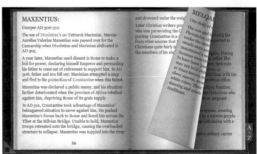

Ethan Haas Was Right & Alpha Omega

"The mystery surrounding this whole
campaign was totally intriguing."
Rob Ford, FWA

Client
Mind Storm Labs

Credits
RED Interactive Agency
www.ff0000.com

Awards
FWA, WebAward, Flash Forward

www.ethanhaaswasright.com
www.alphaomegathegame.com

The Brief

Mind Storm Labs, a role-playing game (RPG) developer, was preparing to launch their first game called "Alpha Omega" (AO). AO is an offline RPG played in the spirit of the classic Dungeons & Dragons game. The plan was to officially introduce and launch the sale of AO at Gen Con, a conference dedicated to gaming culture and its community. For this, Mind Storm Labs had two primary needs. The first was to create an initial buzz and anticipation for the game's release, and the second was to create an official game website that would both promote the game and help expand its base of players.

The Challenge

The first major challenge was to develop a teaser strategy that would help generate excitement for the unknown game before Gen Con. Our timeline totaled a tight four weeks, which included everything from concepting through to the final launch. The second challenge was that most RPG games are so complicated that they often dissuade newcomers from wanting to learn how to play. However, AO was different; it was more fun, adaptive, flexible, and simpler to use. We needed to build the AO online experience to reflect these and other key game characteristics, while also convincing people to invest their time and money in AO. In the end, the campaign had to create enough momentum for a successful game launch and the start of a growing AO customer base.

03 Promotional

The Solution

After thorough research on our target audience, we came up with the concept "Ethan Haas Was Right".

Ethan Haas was a character pulled from the actual back-story of AO: a prophet from the 14th Century who predicted the end of the world in the year 2049. We also created a fictitious current-day game character named Van Mantra, who understood the secret prophesies of Haas and was here to inform those who were sympathetic and worthy of the knowledge.

The teaser site presented an immersive post-apocalyptic environment. Visitors were told nothing upon first arrival. No messages, no clues, no mention of the game. They were confronted with only a series of highly interactive puzzles, which in turn unlocked a series of hidden gritty videos of Van Mantra. These videos continued to offer more back-story, ultimately hinting that a major event was coming on August 1st.

On August 1st, the official game website was launched.

The Results

Visitors spent hours on the teaser site, striving to reach the end; yet no one knew what it was really promoting. This lack of information only fueled more interest and curiosity. The site quickly became viral and spread across the Internet as many gamer communities and newcomers worked in groups to solve the puzzles. Innumerable blogs, Wikipedia, and various news publications (including USA Today and Forbes) picked up word of the campaign. And each one took a guess at what the site was promoting and what would happen on August 1st. When that day finally arrived, the main site launched with much excitement, heavy traffic, and a large dedicated following.

14.5 Million unique visits
(2 months)

75,000 Email sign-ups

8 Minutes average
time on site

UFC

"The site for UFC 75 features a 3-D carousel of fighters! Despite the plethora of carousels out there, this one really looks pretty darn cool. RED Interactive, the company behind these sites, should be applauded for creating some truly stunning Flash work!"
Lee Brimelow, The Flash Blog

The Brief

What used to be an underground attraction has become mainstream. The Ultimate Fighting Championship (UFC) is the fastest growing, and arguably most exciting sport in the world. In an effort to promote UFC Pay-Per-View events, RED was tasked with creating an ongoing campaign to increase awareness, strengthen the fan-base, and drive viewership. This has resulted in the design and development of engaging websites created to appeal to both existing fans and newcomers to the sport. These sites incorporate everything from exciting fighter videos and analysis sections, to polls and historical timelines.

The Challenge

Designing and developing UFC sites is creative and fun, but not without rewarding challenges. Project timelines ranged from two to six weeks and all assets needed to be created from scratch (other than standard fighter photos and event videos). Moreover, there were no prior success stories or case studies to learn from. The UFC was on a rapid public rise and the websites needed to keep up with the pace. Given that virtually every event site is completely unique, we had to continually find new ways to engage targeted users and tell stories that establish an emotional connection with them. Moreover, the sites had to match the incredibly high production value of the actual events, and they needed to satiate the never-ending hunger of UFC fans for new, original content.

03 Promotional

Client
Ultimate Fighting Championship

Credits
RED Interactive Agency
www.ff0000.com

Awards
FWA, WebAward, W3, Pixel Awards

71.ufc.com
75.ufc.com
79.ufc.com
94.ufc.com

The Solution
We created the sites from the mindset of being a fan. Proper time was spent at the beginning of each project to learn about what made each specific event unique. Why should fans want to tune in? What's at stake? What stories should be told? How does this event fit into the big UFC picture? Once the right answers were in hand, the creativity flowed and the sites, one by one, took shape. In order to keep a fresh perspective for each site, there were revolving teams and creative leads that took turns rolling up their sleeves and immersing themselves in the brand.

The Results
The UFC has experienced a constant rate of explosive growth and each piece of the puzzle played a role in that success, including the event sites. These sites typically launched three to four weeks prior to an event, and received anywhere from 150,000 to 500,000 unique visitors during the week of the event alone. User interaction times often ranged between 10 and 25 minutes, and the brand evangelists loudly promote the sites across the social Web. Although UFC Pay-Per-View events cannot be purchased online (they can only be purchased from cable/satellite providers), it's clear that visits to these event sites strongly influence targeted users to make the purchase.

698,000 Unique visits
(1 week)

15:48 Minutes average
time on site

4 Page impressions
per session

Lincoln MKS

"The microsite that was produced for the MKS
literally and figuratively launched Lincoln back
into the minds of consumers and into the luxury
vehicle market as being relevant again."
Ken Tadeo, Creative Director,
Wunderman – Team Detroit

Client
Lincoln

Credits
Wunderman – Team Detroit
www.teamdetroit.com
BLITZ Agency
www.blitzagency.com

Awards
FWA, Webby

http://fit.am/003

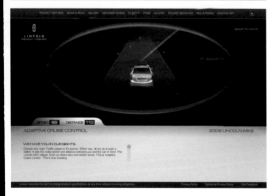

The Brief

For the launch of the Lincoln MKS, Team Detroit wanted to reintroduce Lincoln as a luxury brand, a category that has long been dominated by European vehicles such as BMW, Audi, and Mercedes. In addition to the loyal Lincoln audience, they wanted to generate buzz among a young, affluent group whose focus in cars was not only luxury, but also technology. From a branding perspective, Lincoln was set to launch their new positioning, Reach Higher – a broad transition from their more traditional brand voice, as this utilized a more futuristic style, palette, and tone.

The Challenge

The "luxury" market is, and had been for many years, dominated by nameplate, European brands, leaving American luxury vehicles like Lincoln neglected. This presented a challenge, but also a great opportunity for the brand to reinvent itself as well as establish a new automobile line in the saturated market; one that combined two differentiating attributes that Lincoln had been introducing with their vehicles: luxury and technology.

The Solution

Working with the style created for the offline campaign by Wunderman and Y&R, BLITZ created a futuristic setting that took full advantage of motion, sound, and sleek, seductive design. Advanced technology features, such as adaptive headlamps, adaptive cruise control, and connectivity and multimedia options, were highlighted throughout via interactive vignettes. Additionally, the site included video demonstrations and interviews from Lincoln designers and engineers who spoke about the detail and ingenuity that went into the new techno/luxury line.

The Results

The campaign, and more specifically the site, helped Lincoln become a consideration for luxury shoppers again, exceeding expectations by 32%. During the campaign it garnered over one million unique visitors and a 90% completion rate on the extended video demonstrations, while also being praised by professionals throughout the automotive industry.

1 Million unique users

90 Percent video completion rate

32 Percent expectation increase

Allstate Garage

"The rich media site has been beautifully developed and boasts an online application that allows you to customize your own motorcycle. In 12 steps biking fans can design and create their dreams by choosing between different frames, wheel sets, front-ends, handlebars… Rich in detail, the site is a treat for the eye, even for non-bikers."
Roland Crepeau, culture-buzz.com

The Brief

Allstate Insurance Company had a primary objective of increasing the number of qualified motorcycle insurance leads generated online. In order to meet this objective, our task was to increase awareness of the brand's online quote tool and position Allstate as experts with the best motorcycle coverage on the market.

The Challenge

To create a fully immersive site experience that positions Allstate's motorcycle insurance as both exciting and informative in an unconventional way. We created an experiential video site that featured the mechanics of Indian Larry Legacy, a widely respected custom chopper shop located in New York City. Visitors were given the ability to watch the mechanics build a bike in real time and even build their own custom choppers, comprised of 3-D modeled parts. The site featured gritty graphics and authentic garage-like qualities, from grease stains and pin-ups, to tool chests and hydraulic lifts.

Client
Allstate for Leo Burnett

Credits
Leo Burnett
www.leoburnett.com
Domani Studios
www.domanistudios.com

Awards
FWA, Webby, HOW, IMA, Davey,
WMA, W3, Cannes

http://allstate.dev.domanistudios.com

35,000 Quote leads

10 Minutes average time on site

80,000 Bikes created

45,000 Wallpapers created

The Solution

Site visitors were given several channels in which to interact with Allstate agents and the insurance quote tool. A constant, well-designed "Get a Quote" call to action was prominently placed within the main navigation and artfully built into each main site area. Within a single click, users could enter their zip code, which then deep-linked them directly into the first step of the online quoting system. The Garage also featured a "Find an Agent" tool, which allowed users to enter their zip codes and thus return a list of agents in their area.

In an effort to bring the consumer closer to the agents and Allstate team, we created our custom "Plan a Ride" route planner, which utilized the Google Maps API, to feature some of the most well-known rides across the country and give users the ability to plot and save their own routes to share with the rest of the biking community. Our team also built an events calendar, displaying all of the stops along the Allstate Mobile Garage tour, which made its way to every major motorcycle rally across the US, providing safety seminars and showcasing celebrity mechanics and their famous bikes.

The site housed a wealth of safety tips and insurance coverage information, including a "Garage TV" section, which contained a video player full of informative tips courtesy of Allstate and the boys over at Indian Larry Legacy. These clips were also launched on to their own YouTube channel, further extending the reach of the Allstate Garage brand within the online community.

The Results

Since Allstate Garage first opened its metal-plated door, it has won numerous interactive accolades and industry praise, including awards from the Cannes Lions International Advertising Festival, Webbys, Creativity, Communication Arts, and garnering FWA's Site of The Day honors.

The site has generated over 35,000 quote leads and the Build a Bike feature has maintained over ten minutes of brand interaction time, per user, per visit. Over 80,000 bikes have been saved to the Build a Bike gallery and over 45,000 desktop wallpapers have been downloaded, ensuring Allstate's brand presence well beyond the initial site visit.

After seeing how users so positively reacted to the route planner and bike building applications, Allstate instituted an internal policy, calling for agents to use the site as a marketing and customer relationship tool. Agents create a route or a bike via the site and then use the built-in send-to-friend email functionality to send personal and/or blasted messages out to customers sharing their favorite routes or latest creation. Campaign success has continued well beyond launch and added features continue to be introduced to the site as its influence and effectiveness evolves.

M&M's Join the Hunt

"Someone will be doing their regular
online searches or surfing the net, when
all of a sudden they'll come across
an egg. This element of surprise will
certainly keep the momentum."
John Gagne, Vice-President,
Creative Director, Proximity Canada

Client
Mars Canada

Credits
Proximity Canada
www.proximity.ca
Firstborn
www.firstbornmultimedia.com

Awards
FWA

www.jointhehunt.ca

The Brief
On behalf of Mars Canada, Proximity Canada approached Firstborn to collaborate on the Web component of an M&M's spring campaign called "Join the Hunt". The "hunt" is a nation-wide egg hunt designed to promote the seasonal sales of the speckled, egg-shaped M&M's candies. The campaign drives consumers to find and collect PIN codes hidden online and inside specially marked packages of M&M's Speck-tacular eggs. Each PIN code is worth a certain number of points and the more points a user redeems, the better their chances of winning thousands of instant prizes or one of the three grand prize getaways to New York, Las Vegas, or Orlando.

The Challenge
Mars Canada wanted to leverage the fun and sharing associated with the Easter occasion to steal share from Cadbury, drive awareness and incremental sales growth of M&M's Speck-tacular Eggs, and increase purchase frequency. The overarching challenge was to create a campaign that clears the way for M&M's Speck-tacular eggs to take over as the chocolate treat of choice at Easter. In the original client ask, the website was to exist as a means for users to create a profile and keep track of their point totals. However, while the key purpose of this campaign was to drive physical package sales, both agencies felt strongly that the online presence should draw the user deeper into the experience of the campaign – that the concept should expand beyond in-pack PINs to literally create an egg hunt across the Web.

03 Promotional

The Solution

The solution was a multimedia promotion that crosses boundaries between online and offline with JoinTheHunt.ca as the centerpiece of the campaign. On the site, users can enter PIN codes collected through purchase, as well as continue to hunt online with the help of Red and Yellow for more chances to win. Dozens of eggs are hidden throughout four intricate environments within the site, but we also developed four interactive games placed throughout the experience and purchased external domain names for which mini websites were created to hide even more eggs for more chances to win. To encourage purchase frequency, several in-pack PIN codes offered the extra bonus of a chance at instant win prizes in addition to Grand Prize entries. The amount of hidden content online is directly proportional to the amount of time spent on the site and the experience truly provides an engaging environment through which users can really interact with the brand. Along with online media, the program was further supported by brand and promotional TV spots and in-store POS to drive overall awareness.

The Results

After launching the site, the average user-time in April 2009 onward has been over 16 minutes and the number of registered users actively entering in PINs is over 34,000. Another result of the site was the leveraging of the digital assets created for the TV spot. Because we created so much 3-D for the site (including Red and Yellow) we were able to use these assets to develop a TV spot, helping save budget and time.

462,000 — Total PIN codes submitted

34,000 — Total registrations

16 — Minutes average time on site

Microsoft Clearification

"I rarely can find cool and innovative
things that Microsoft pulls off, but
geez… huge props on this."
The Apple Blog, from the post
'Microsoft Does Something Hip'

Client
Microsoft

Credits
Mekanism
www.mekanism.com
McCann Worldgroup
www.mccannsf.com

Awards
FWA, Cannes, LIA, Webby, Clio, D&AD,
One Show, AAF

http://clearification.mekanism.com

The Brief

The brief was one word: Clarity.

The new Windows Vista operating system promised to act as your digital hub and allow a cleaner and easier user experience.

So our initiative was to create a positive online buzz for Windows Vista in a manner that was low-key and unexpected from Microsoft. The young audience was already skeptical of the brand, so any communication or engagement with the brand had to be done in *their* world, not shouting at them from outside of it.

The Challenge

How do you create credible word-of-mouth buzz for a brand that was seen as "old" and the absolute opposite of "hip"? And how do you do so with no substantial media dollars? Microsoft needed to find some way to showcase their brand new, much more stylish yet easy-to-use operating system to a world of consumers who just didn't believe they were capable of such a thing. Essentially, Microsoft had to start from square one in terms of losing their infamous "square" stigma.

5 — Million total viewers

1.2 — Million site visits

1.5 — Million syndicated video views

50,500 Google results

The Solution
We enlisted indie hipster Demetri Martin to create a brand story woven across broadcast spots, the clearification.com website, a live comedy tour, short films, and a one-hour special on Comedy Central. Seeding the short films on user-generated-content sites and online social networks, we drove users to clearification.com creating a large integrated buzz campaign. The episodic story follows Demetri as he attempts to un-clutter his life and find clarity. It begins, as most stories do, with Episode One entitled: "A Rare Condition". After that, as one would also expect, there were five more episodes with silly names. But that was the point: get Microsoft to be seen as a brand that doesn't take itself TOO seriously, and let people have fun with the brand again. And silly names help that. So does the world's first puppet blog.

The Results
User-generated-content sites YouTube, Google Video, MSN, AtomFilms, iFilm, Revver, and dozens more delivered over one million views throughout the six-month campaign, igniting massive word-of-mouth across the blogosphere and social networks, driving millions of unique users to the website. Beyond that, the comedy special was the highest-rated show in its time slot and the campaign was a huge success story for Microsoft. Did it change the mind of the consumer about the brand? As one user stated, "If anyone can make Windows Vista or Microsoft cool, it's Demetri Martin." Well put, and we'd have to agree looking at the results.

Criss Angel: Mindfreak

"EVB pulls off a multi-platform magic trick
that plunges users into the unbelievable
illusions of A&E's 'Criss Angel Mindfreak.'"
ON: Digital + Marketing

WANT MORE CRISS ANGEL?
Terms of Service   Privacy Statement

The Brief

Criss Angel is a modern-day Houdini who performs crazy illusions and magic tricks on stages in Las Vegas and on his A&E Networks cable show, "Criss Angel: Mindfreak." He maintains a fan club of "ultimate loyal freaks", but the show's appeal needed to be broadened. The solution? Create an online experience with viral appeal to build anticipation for his show's season premiere. The idea had to be as "mystical" as the man himself: literally freak people's minds and gain tremendous levels of involvement and pass-along value.

The Challenge

A&E had high hopes for the third season of "Mindfreak". Criss' popularity was on the rise and the network knew that they had an opportunity to leverage his notoriety to drive viewership and increase ratings for the show's premiere. They approached EVB with a simple challenge: "develop a campaign that will get people to tune in to the premiere of 'Criss Angel: Mindfreak'."

No creative approach or execution was mandated. EVB was given the latitude to come back with any idea that could work in any media or platform. With a modest budget and very little paid media support, the agency knew that we needed to focus on an idea that was big enough and engaging enough that it would make noise and create buzz on a national level.

Client
A&E Networks

Credits
Evolution Bureau (EVB)
http://evb.com

Awards
FWA, D&AD

http://mindfreak.evb-archive.com

The Solution

At his core, Criss Angel is a charismatic performer and an incredible illusionist. We tapped into both of these traits to create Freakyourmind.com.

The goal of the site was to create an illusion that was very personal to each visitor, but could also work on a mass scale. This is how it worked: the user would go to freakyourmind.com where they were asked to select their friend's name from an extensive pre-recorded list and input their friend's phone number. The friend would then receive an email disguised as an unbranded random "YouTube-type" video link. The link would lead the user to a seemingly passive and innocuous video of Criss Angel. This is where the fun started.

After drawing you in with a brief set-up, Criss asks you to close your eyes and picture the letters in your name. Then, to the utter amazement of the viewer, he correctly guesses your name and pulls out a deck of cards and proceeds to lay them out on a table in the order of your phone number. It doesn't stop there. Two minutes later, your phone rings and Criss greets you by name and requests that you watch the season premiere of his show.

This "illusion" was created by pre-recording hundreds of names, shooting video of every variable from multiple angles, and dynamically stitching the whole thing together in Flash and integrating the mobile element, to create a seamless experience. Of course, its success also had a lot to do with a stellar performance by Criss Angel.

The Results

Engagement numbers for this site were incredibly high proving that the use of truly breakthrough concept and technology escalated momentum to the mainstream. Over the next 30 days, nearly three million people created a customized video to play a joke on their friends. More importantly, the idea delivered on its primary objective and drove viewership. The premiere of "Criss Angel: Mindfreak" was the highest-rated cable show in its time slot, beating out the season finale of "The Shield". It also became the highest-rated Mindfreak episode of all time.

03 Promotional

3 Million users in three weeks

9,000 Blog mentions

Social Media

04

A not quite long time ago in a faraway land, there existed a feudal system of Publishers who sought to control the largest number of Users as their loyal subjects. (Archeologists would later refer to this prehistoric era as Web 1.0.) Users were happy for a while until one day they discovered that they, too, could become Publishers – quite easily in fact – and form their own kingdoms and communities.

They created a new land where content is democratized and where each User could become their own king. New social websites and services soon enabled them to publish royal decrees (called Blogs and Podcasts), vote for content they Digg, discover old friends on Social Networks, Poke (and even SuperPoke) each other, become Internet Famous, gain Followers, and in a few cases, become even larger and more powerful than the great Publisher kingdoms of yore. They named this new utopia Web 2.0 and immediately started to blog about how cliché the name was. Welcome to the Social Web.

"They named this new utopia Web 2.0 and immediately started to blog about how cliché the name was."

Take a deep breath and dive beneath the hype and hyperbole, the latest social app or iPhone widget, the memes and micro-celebrities, and there discover a powerful riptide that is rapidly altering the basic fundamentals of human society. Never before have so many gained so much power to express, collaborate, and connect on such a global scale. It's not just that it's possible for a few celebrities with million-dollar smiles or media conglomerates with billion-dollar satellites, it's that it's easy for nearly anyone nowadays to network like jetsetters and publish globally in a few clicks of a mouse, usually for free, and often without even realizing it.

Importantly, it's not that any one website or technology is enabling this change, but rather that there's a growing intersection of many different social websites and services that are focused on making it easy for users to easily express themselves (Publishing), enabling them to rapidly connect with others and interact with content (Participation), and putting the user at the center of attention (Personalization).

Publishing by the people used to be an expensive, esoteric affair, from the quill pen and the savant, to the webserver and the hacker. But new Web services made it free (mostly) and accessible for anyone to publish whatever they want, wherever they want to whomever they want; services like Flickr (photos), YouTube (videos), and MySpace (music and the people themselves).

Participation is the power that drives democracies, movements, and all organizations. Social websites like Digg made it possible for people to vote for their favorite content and news, empowering people to become democratic editors of mass media – a dramatic role reversal of the couch potato. Social networks like Facebook and LinkedIn helped people connect with each other, ignoring the usual laws of time (often automatically connecting you with people far away and long forgotten from high school) and space (forming groups with people all over the world).

"Participation is the power that drives democracies, movements, and all organizations."

Personalization represents the most fundamental of human needs, ownership, and individuality. Personalized startpages like Netvibes enable people to recreate their own version of the Web, gathering all their favorite blogs, news sites, social networks, and widgets all in one place that reflects who they are. New personalized services give people a sense of ownership and of being at the center of a service built just for them, such as Pandora and Last.fm (personalized music), Wikis (notes and articles that anyone can edit), and My Times (personalized New York Times).

It's not a coincidence that sites in each stage include the properties and abilities of those that preceded it. Publishing created an explosion of user-generated content and empowered everyone with a voice. Next, Participation gave birth to crowdsourcing and social networking, which require both the topics (content) and the ability to discuss them (freedom of speech) brought about by Publishing. Finally, in our latest evolution, Personalization services are now making it easier to Participate and Publish in more channels and more ways without fatigue, with widgets and semantic technologies that tailor the entire Web and deliver it to them exactly the way they want it.

No wonder that the most successful examples of social websites manage to fulfil all three promises to users. Wikipedia, an encyclopedia where anyone can contribute and edit content, participate in discussions and debates, and publish in many different languages and countries around the world – powered by its millions of users – in just a few short years has created an online encyclopedia that's many times larger in content (and some would argue more accurate), more widely distributed, and cheaper (free) than the incumbent Encyclopedia Britannica (which took 200 years to secure its throne).

04 Social Media

This illustrates one important problem the social Web has brought upon us: the plight of newspapers and print publishers who are struggling to find their role in a world where everyone is also a publisher and, therefore, a competitor. Another issue is that of information overload and endless requests for their attention: billions of blog articles, friend requests, group invitations, status updates, and activity feeds, and tempting invitations to try the latest new site of the day. It's hard enough to maintain a real life, let alone a virtual profile across dozens of services and groups across the Web. Finally, let us not forget that brands and advertisers have an even more daunting task now that society has entered the largest attention deficit in human history.

"The case studies that follow are among the founding fathers and mothers, and passionate new innovators of Web 2.0 that will serve as blueprints for the brave new Web to follow."

True, this can all start to sound pretty melodramatic pretty quickly, which perhaps points out the biggest change of all: that we as individuals have put at the center of everything, the center of the world. And if the world is our oyster, it will come to us on a silver platter. We can already see a trend in this direction in the ironic death of the social website as a destination and its diffusion across the Web as a distributed service in the form of an RSS feed or widget that's personalized and delivered to us. It's good to be a User, it's good to be the king – and it's going to get even better.

Who knows what will happen to the land of Publishers and Users (perhaps they are already becoming one). But the case studies that follow are among the founding fathers and mothers, and passionate new innovators of Web 2.0 that will serve as blueprints, or at least genetic markers, for the brave new Web to follow.

Freddy Mini
Netvibes

Bio.
Freddy Mini
Netvibes

Freddy Mini is CEO of Netvibes,
the leading personalized
startpage and widget
marketing platform, serving
more than 1,000 of the world's
top agencies, brands, and
publishers. Freddy is a leading
expert on user personalization
marketing and widget
technology strategies for
global brands and publishers.

Prior to Netvibes, he was the
co-founder of musicMe (the
first music search service),
CEO of Ziff Davis (France),
and Senior VP and Managing
Director of CNET Networks
Europe where he was
responsible for creating and
expanding regional operations
to more than 150 people while
exceeding all profitability goals.
–
www.netvibes.com

"Never before have
so many gained
so much power to
express, collaborate,
and connect on such
a global scale."

Netvibes

"Netvibes is like the iWeb for brands and marketers.
It was great to see our team jump in and just start testing
ideas, instead of waiting on developers to code it for
them. We just picked the widgets we wanted, placed
them where we wanted and we were done – seven city
travel guides published in less than a month's time."
Josué Macle, Co-Managing Director,
Duke Interactive London

The Brief

Netvibes was created as an alternative to the traditional search portal to help people gain control over their digital lives. Netvibes brings together all your favorite parts of the Web – blogs, news, social networks, widgets, and friends – all in one place. Today, Netvibes comprises a network of millions of users in more than 100 countries and 80 languages, each with their own unique and personalized version of their Web. By ushering in a new era of user personalization, Netvibes also pioneered the concept of *personalization marketing*, enabling thousands of brands, marketers, and media companies to go far beyond one-way advertising by engaging social consumers with useful widgets and branded portals.

The Challenge

While Web 2.0 led to a golden explosion of social media, user-generated content, and new services, it also brought with it the problems of information overload and search fatigue. Not only were users finding it hard to surf and sort through the Web, but brands were also finding it more difficult to get their messages heard and engage these users. Traditional search and display advertising both started to prove insufficient in the new, much larger social Web. It was apparent that a single, "one size fits all" Web would be insufficient to hold all this content while remaining efficient and relevant enough for people and businesses to use every day. A new user-personalized Web, an alternative to traditional search portals and display advertising, was needed.

Client
Netvibes and 1,000+ brands

Credits
Ogilvy
www.ogilvy.com
Duke Interactive
– A Razorfish company
www.duke-interactive.com
Advertising Research Foundation
www.thearf.org

Awards
TechCrunch 50, Time magazine 50 Best Websites, PC World 100, Business 2.0, Webware 100, AlwaysOn Media 100, Red Herring 100, MIT Tech Review TR35, SEOMoz Web 2.0 Award, Webuser, Dutch Web2.0 Award

http://business.netvibes.com

Social Media
Netvibes

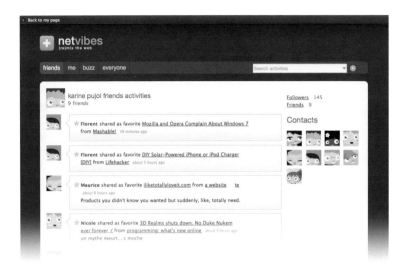

The Solution

In 2005, Netvibes launched as the world's most personalizable startpage: no ads, no logos, and no surfing. Instead of going out every day to search the Web to visit their favorite sites and services, Netvibes delivered it directly to them. Netvibes was the first to partner with 1,600+ media companies to make RSS syndication accessible and engaging to everyday consumers. Translation tools allowed Netvibes to crowdsource its localization into more than 100 countries in less than a year. For brands and marketers, Netvibes pioneered a universal widget platform, instant widget creation and drag-and-drop personalized microsite publishing tools, and widget syndication services to help better engage social consumers within the personalized Web, without advertising.

The Results

By building a new and more personalized Web, Netvibes has attracted millions of users, thousands of media partners, hundreds of leading brands, marketing agencies, and large enterprises, and dozens of awards and accolades. Today, top marketers and brands around the world are using Netvibes to build and distribute universal widgets and personalized microsite portals, and build long-term relationships with consumers on the Web.

181,000 Widgets

10,000 Community developers

1,600 Media partners & brands

100 Countries reached

9 Month widget lifespan

Candystand

"Kudos to Candystand.com for creating a series
of branded offerings that seem able to stand
alone in the gaming world. It hasn't been
an easy trek, considering Candystand was
first introduced in '97 – building this kind of
recognition takes time. Just ask Target."
Angela Natividad, Adrants.com

The Brief

Candystand.com has been one of the leading free online game sites since its inception in 1997. The site has steadily grown over the years, now featuring over 150 unique, high-quality games in a variety of genres, all with a family friendly appeal. Since 2005, WDDG has managed, designed, and maintained the site and game catalog for the Wm. Wrigley Jr. Company. In the fall of 2008, WDDG formed the Funtank company and acquired Candystand.com.

The Challenge

Candystand.com had enjoyed a great amount of success as a branded entertainment portal when Funtank acquired the property in the fall of 2008, but there were a number of challenges it was facing. Traffic had been steadily declining due to increased competition in the rapidly emerging online gaming market. Competitive sites were launching more games, and at a faster pace. The site would be opening up to other advertisers, so advertising inventory would need to be created for these new advertisers to take advantage of. And finally, the site's then-current design was over three years old, predating many of the advances that came with the Web 2.0 revolution. Essentially the challenge boiled down to re-growing the site's traffic, monetizing that traffic to its full potential, and bringing the site up to speed with current trends in design and technology.

Client
WDDG/Funtank

Credits
WDDG
www.wddg.com
Funtank
www.funtank.com

www.candystand.com

The Solution

WDDG/Funtank attacked these challenges in multiple phases. The first phase concentrated on rebuilding traffic and awareness, rethinking the game schedule, and incorporating advertising units across the site. The game pipeline was greatly increased, targeting a release schedule of close to one new game per week. We took a deep look at organic search-engine performance, optimizing the site for SEO, particularly Google. After these tweaks to the site were completed, the team immediately began on the next phase: the full redesign of not only the site, but the Candystand brand. To position the site for further and future growth, Funtank overhauled the entire user experience, incorporating the best practices of Web 2.0, APIs from key social networks, and advances in technology. The branding was completely redesigned to target our audience better – gamers of all ages and genders, but keying in on the teen and tween audiences.

The Results

We'd like to let the stats do the talking: (all of these are from the first six months – September 1, 2008 to March 1, 2009)

• Monthly Unique Visitors up 67%
• Monthly Total Visits up 53%
• Monthly Page-views up 45%
• Monthly Google Referrals up 73.6 %
• Monthly Search Engine Traffic up 60%
• Monthly Visits from referring sites up 80%

10.5

Million monthly
site visits

5

Million unique
visitors per month

44

Million monthly
page-views

7:49

Minutes average
time on site

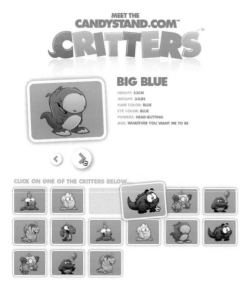

Last.fm

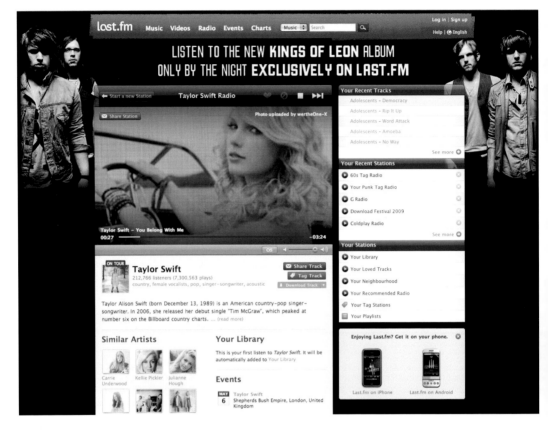

"Music Non Stop."
Martin Stiksel,
Co-Founder, Last.fm

The Brief

As part of his degree project at Southampton University, Richard Jones started tracking what he and his friends were listening to on their computers with a project he called Audioscrobbler. At the same time, Felix Miller and Martin Stiksel, who were running an online record label, had a vision for personalized radio that learns what you like. They were streaming music from a small website, but when the three eventually met, they merged their ideas, and bam, scrobble data was put to use feeding the Last.fm recommendation engine. The two sites became fully integrated in 2003.

The Challenge

These days there is more music available online than ever before – much of it free and only some of it legal – which means help is all the more vital, as most listeners don't have the time or inclination to sift through it all. They want recommendations that are easy to access and make sense to their taste (in other words, not just a handful of reviewers telling them what's hot or not). So the question was: how to provide trustworthy recommendations that would resonate with the widest spectrum of users? From hip-hop to country to rock'n'roll, from Top 40 fans to long-tailers who pride themselves on the obscure. On top of that, keep in mind that even online listeners consume music in many ways – Internet radio stations, music videos, CDs, iTunes singles, etc.

Client
Last.fm

Credits
Last.fm development team
www.last.fm

Awards
UK Digital Music Award, Mashable,
Chip Award, and others

www.last.fm

04 Social Media

30 Million unique
users a month

1 Billion tracks scrobbled
per month

45 Million tracks
in catalogue

300,000 Artists and labels

600,000 Free mp3s

The Solution

The answer lay in the music community itself. After all, who better to tap for recommendations than other active listeners? Especially those whose taste overlaps with yours. With that in mind, Last.fm takes scrobbling technology and combines it with a social network of passionate music fans. We use collaborative filtering (i.e. people who like x also like y) and social recommendations to surface new discoveries based on music you've told the site you like. And it scales – the more you listen, the more of your music is scrobbled; and with more data to work from, the scrobbler can produce even better results. Same goes for others in your community – the more they scrobble, the more accurate your recommendations become. The final piece was presentation. To make this data usable we've created a library of over 12 million artist pages that include song streams and downloads, album data, bios, photos, videos, news feeds, and event information. We filter artists by genre and user-generated tags, create personalized radio, and generate charts to help surface relevant content.

The Results

The results are, frankly, astounding. As of early 2009, Last.fm claimed more than 30 million unique users per month, an impressive 89% of whom came back at least once a week. With numbers like that, it's clear that scrobbling has been useful. And it continues to be: one billion tracks are scrobbled each month – approximately 500 every second.

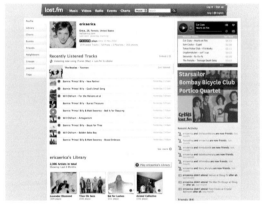

Flock, the Social Browser

"As the browser market and the social space
mature we're seeing a natural evolution
toward better options for consumers."
Shawn Hardin, CEO of Flock

Client
Flock

Credits
Flock
www.flock.com
K/F Communications
www.kfcomm.com

Awards
Webby, SXSW, PC World's 100,
MacWorld Eddy

www.flock.com

The Brief

Flock is the only browser designed to let active, social Web users stay connected to the friends and content they care about, directly from the browser. Flock lets them keep their finger on the pulse of their social networks, yet gives them unprecedented freedom to explore online without having to click back and forth between social networks, web mail, media, news feeds, and blogs. Flock also helps users share and publish content efficiently to multiple locations at once. And Flock is also the only browser that allows users to take Facebook Chat with them wherever they go on the Internet. Flock is now used in over 14,000 cities and over 192 countries and territories. Flock is free to download and use at http://www.flock.com.

The Challenge

People are spending more time on the Web as it has become increasingly interactive and engaging. At the same time, it has become more fragmented which makes it difficult for users to effectively manage multiple identities and accounts across numerous locations. They want to have the freedom to wander the Internet and find the information that is the most interesting and relevant to them, and then share it with the people they care about. Yet as the number of social networks, web mail, media, news feeds, and blogs proliferate at lightning speed, so does the concern that users are not keeping up with content and friends. This social network stress leads to fatigue. It is increasing and only promises to worsen as the amount of information, applications, and online friends grow.

04 Social Media

The Solution

Stay up to date with what social network friends are doing using Flock's People Sidebar. Make searching and sharing photos and videos easily accessible in the Media Bar. Drag and drop photos, articles, videos – anything they want to share – directly on to a friend's profile, into an email, or directly into their blog. Share and discover content via Twitter. Simply drag and drop URLs, photos, videos, text, or other content to a friend's Twitter, Facebook, MySpace or other profile in Flock's People Sidebar. With Twitter Search, save your Twitter searches in one place.

FlockCast capability allows for the instant "broadcast" of public actions to multiple locations at once. Post and promote personal blogs into Facebook effortlessly. Simply drag and drop content found anywhere on the Web into blogs and Flock broadcasts it to the Facebook news-feed. Also automatically post Twitter status updates to Facebook and upload photos to Flickr, Photobucket, and Picasa. Easily track, update, and organize RSS feeds in one place.

The Results

Flock keeps its users in touch with over 500,000,000 friends who are loaded into the people sidebar each month. Flock, which pioneered one-click favorites, has made it easier for Users to access their favorite sites over 208,000,000 times since the release of v1.0. Users have engaged with MyWorld over 116,000,000 times.

80,000,000 service accounts have been logged into, including over 2,600,000 Account Sign-ups across the 22 services integrated within Flock. 34,000,000 feeds have been accessed via Flock's Feeds Sidebar. 18,000,000 media streams have been loaded in Flock's Media Bar. 8,500,000 photos and videos have been accessed in the media bar.

Over 8,000,000 photos have been uploaded. Close to 1,000,000 blog posts have been made with Flock.

400
Percent user growth

7.5
Million downloads

71
Percent use Flock as primary browser

4
Hours average use per day

90
Percent word-of-mouth adoption

04 Social Media

Red Bull Flugtag Flight Lab

"I'm in awe. This is a truly incredible use
of the engine, or any Flash 3D engine for
that matter. The overall implementation
is incredible. Truly awesome work."
Ralph Hauwert, Core Dev-Team
of Papervision3D

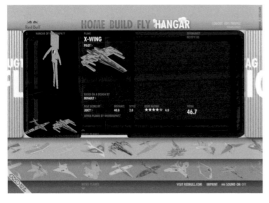

The Brief

Less Rain always had an interest in tools, toys, and games that allow users to get creative online. When Red Bull asked us to come up with new ways to interact with the brand, we proposed several ideas revolving around the concept of creative multi-user applications – after all, Red Bull supposedly stimulates the mind too, not just the body.

The Red Bull Flugtag event was an ideal contender to base such a tool on. With its focus on fun and creativity and the broad audience it attracts we felt that this event was particularly well suited for translating it into a creative online activity.

The Challenge

The first challenge for us was to find an adequate translation of Red Bull Flugtag, that without trying to imitate would still remain faithful to the spirit of the event. A logical addition was, for example, to let users share their creations online, and let everyone use and also modify everyone else's aeroplanes.

But the main challenge of course was the actual technical implementation. The Red Bull Flugtag Flight Lab was the first commercial project of this size to utilise the Papervision3D engine, which especially in its early stages was not very well documented and subject to some major revisions.

From translating a freehand drawing into a 3-dimensional aeroplane model with realistic physical properties, to modifying a physics engine to model birds rather than planes, to simulating a water "surface" for the plane to crash into, the project was never short on challenges for us to solve.

Client
Red Bull

Credits
Less Rain
www.lessrain.com

Awards
FWA, BIMA, Davey Awards, W3 Awards, One Show Entertainment, Cannes, European Design Award, FAB Awards, Clio Awards, One Show Interactive, Flash in the Can, Interactive Media Awards, BombShock, Adobe

www.redbull.com/flightlab

04 Social Media

The Solution
Before the project was green-lighted by the client we developed two prototypes as proof of concept. One for the building tool, and one for the actual game.

The prototypes didn't solve all problems we encountered, but they showed the technical feasibility. And by the time the actual production began we already had a good understanding of the project as a whole.

We divided Flight Lab into several discreet parts that could be developed simultaneously by different teams across all our offices: the building tool, painting tool, channel navigation, high-score tables, the game, and so on, and then later assembled all these pieces into the website framework.

The Results
Throughout the year, Red Bull hosts Flugtag events across the globe, and for every event Flight Lab can be utilised as traffic driver.

The site has received unanimous praise worldwide, by consumers, gamers, and the Web design community alike. Spreading virally just through word of mouth, it appeared quickly on thousands of blogs, ranging from the Web design community to model plane enthusiasts, and was featured in numerous print publications.

Flight Lab increased traffic on RedBull. com three-fold immediately after launch, and is one year later still responsible for almost half the traffic.

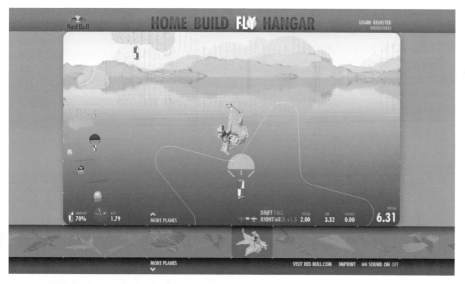

9 — Minutes average
time on site

8,000 — Aeroplanes
designed

34 — Hours longest
air-time by a player

FVA: The Favourite Visitor Awards

"I have the BIGGEST smile on my face right now! This is one of those truly exciting moments. What an amazing job you guys have done, I can't thank you all enough!"
Rob Ford, FWA (as client)

Client
FWA: The Favourite Website Awards

Credits
Domani Studios
www.domanistudios.com

www.thefwa.com/50million

The Brief

The Favourite Website Awards (FWA) is a global-industry recognized award program and inspiration portal that offers daily awards for best-in-class websites. The awards are highly coveted within the international design community. The FWA has been growing in popularity steadily since its inception in May 2000 and was about to reach its 50 millionth visit in late April of 2009. To commemorate this milestone the FWA approached Domani Studios (DS), completely open to any ideas of how to highlight this achievement.

The Challenge

To mark this milestone the FWA offered an open invitation to Domani Studios to celebrate the achievement in whatever way was deemed appropriate. The challenge here was that the FWA's core audience is comprised mainly of interactive creatives, who can be a notoriously critical crowd – so promoting the milestone while entertaining them would be demanding.

The Solution

DS proposed that the FWA be flipped on its head and celebrate the "visitor" for a change. To do this, the FWA was "hijacked" for a week, redirecting users unknowingly from the FWA to the FVA (Favourite Visitor Awards). Upon which, the site was taken over by falling balloons, flashing signs, and applause. All of the tiles on the FWA that normally display the Site of the Day winners were replaced with the faces of the FWA visitors.

A snarky M.C. in a ruffled tux helped throw down the celebration and invited users to add themselves to the "Wall of Fame" via the simplicity of Facebook Connect. In effect, the site surprised, congratulated, and then humbly thanked the visitors that make the FWA possible by giving them the chance to be the ones celebrated and viewed by millions.

The Results

Word quickly spread through the Internet of the takeover, creating a huge level of word-of-mouth interest and inciting positive conversations across the blogosphere. The first 24 hours netted the site over 100,000 views and over 1,500 fans added to the wall. All of the share features, such as Facebook Connect and "ShareThis", helped effectively to spread word further, across Facebook, Twitter, and other social-media outlets.

100,000
Visits in the first 24 hours

400,000
Videos played

7,529
Hours of video play-time

6,300
Fans uploaded in ten days

4
Terabytes of bandwidth in ten days

LRPD Vandalsquad

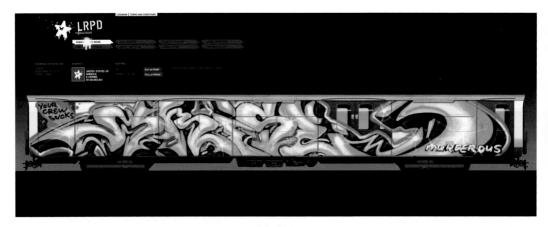

"Vandalsquad, where no talent toys talk shit
& act hard on the internet since 1997."
SPY 1 *SR*RCK*PSC*NET*,
Vandal Squad user

Client
Less Rain (self-initiated)

Credits
Less Rain
www.lessrain.com

Awards
FWA, Macromedia

www.vandalsquad.com

The Brief
It was always our ambition to keep the kids off the street and instead let them explore the world from the comfort of their council estate, using means of modern telecommunication that can be easily supervised and regulated.

In an effort to minimise the kids' desire to disturb the outside world with their presence we recreated virtual renditions of meeting places popular amongst minors, such as a lounge, a disco, a seedy back alley, and a deserted train-yard.

This project, named the "click2music" chat, was commissioned by BMG in 2001. Here, youngsters could create a 3-dimensional likeness of themselves, a so-called "avatar", and then engage in safe, monitored conversation about their favourite pop music acts.

The Challenge
To keep the youngsters' minds occupied we created a series of safe, educational activities inside the click2music chat, such as conjointly listening to music, or the supervised painting of still lives and nature scenes.

However, it was quickly discovered that the tools provided were instead abused for acts of vandalism. Especially in the train-yard area, click2music users would repeatedly paint explicit images or leave threatening messages questioning authority and regulation.

Ultimately, the click2music project closed down when BMG underwent a restructuring process, possibly as a result of their failure to control the young customers effectively.

04 Social Media

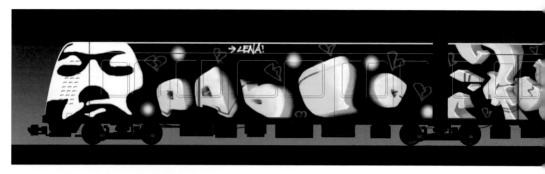

250,000 — Unique users per month

55,000 — Registered users

100,000 — Uploads per month

3 — Million graffiti works hosted

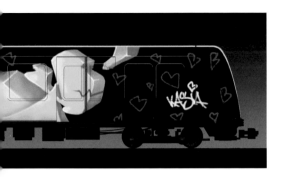

The Solution

We realised that today's youth will not listen to parents or reason or the BMG any more. Failing with being Mister Nice Guy we brought in the bad cop, and by 2004 we established the Less Rain Police Department, or LRPD, with its special task force, the Vandal Squad.

Vandal Squad took over the remains of the click2music chat and developed it into a full-blown educational resort, where the budding graffiti "artists" could undergo several training modules and be re-integrated into the online society.

The Results

With its authoritative voice (and brute force where necessary), the LRPD Vandal Squad quickly became one of the largest online graffiti crime units.

Thousands and thousands of vandals are photographed and registered on the site. They learn about the dangers of graffiti through realistic simulations of the crime. Evidence of the cathartic experience is collected in "black books" for future reference, or uploaded to online TV station "YouTube", an equally safe and heavily controlled environment currently popular among the younger generation.

Today, Vandal Squad is the leading online crime repository and educational environment of its kind, helping to recognise graffiti as an act of dangerous vandalism and not a harmless or even "valuable" form of street art, which is what many of the vandals falsely claim.

04 Social Media

Level-UP!

"Preloaded created a truly innovative experience in what was our first multi-platform outing. A huge success that has resulted in an Interactive BAFTA win."
Siobhan Mulholland,
Senior Producer, CBBC

Client
Children's BBC

Credits
Preloaded
www.preloaded.com

Awards
BAFTA

http://levelup.wedonicethings.com

The Brief
Level-UP! was commissioned as both a television programme and a website for children between the ages of six and twelve. As a 360-degree broadcast/Web experience, the website needed to drive visitors to the show and vice versa, the objective being for the site to encourage these interactions through features such as games, community interaction, and user-generated content, all aimed at an audience for which privacy and safety on-line are paramount.

The Challenge
Developing a 360-degree experience requires a huge amount of planning with all relevant parties so our concept for the site had to be developed with other stakeholders collaboratively. As such we were careful to input into the nature and structure of the TV show which included choosing the name Level Up for the show. Additionally we needed to consider how young children would interact with the site and what content would appeal to them, so user experience was vital to get right, especially when working within a full Flash environment.

Social Media
Level-UP!

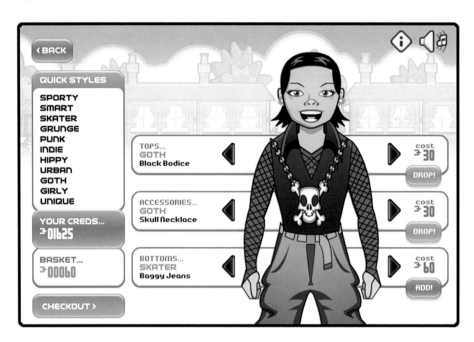

266

The Solution

The site and television programme were developed concurrently, meaning that many features designed for online transferred to broadcast. This ensured an important synergy between the two that was key to guaranteeing the success of both. Viewers of the television programme were encouraged to take part in online activities, with a selection of engaging tools acting as the conduit for the interaction between the show and site. Children could vote on current issues and help others solve everyday problems by supporting each other with helpful advice and tips.

Key to personalisation at the site was an avatar builder within a virtual PDA. Each child was able to customise these to suit their personality and then use the PDA to keep track of their activities and friends. To encourage repeat visits and interaction, players earned points for activities which could be used to purchase a range of items to customise their avatar and PDA. Integration with BBC systems ensured that all progress was saved so children could pick up where they left off on their next visit. To ensure that the site delivered on its remit of encouraging good citizenship, all games were built around civic responsibility. Players were rewarded for being community-minded and helping others, unlike the more traditional destructive take of many games aimed at younger audiences.

The Results

The Level-UP! site quickly became one of the most successful sites at the BBC to make use of their Single Sign-On system, far surpassing the numbers set by other SSO sites. Over the 13-week run the show was broadcast, the site achieved over half a million registered users between six and 13 years of age.

500,000 Registrations

13 Minutes user-time on site

8 Design/development team members

267

Cranium POP 5

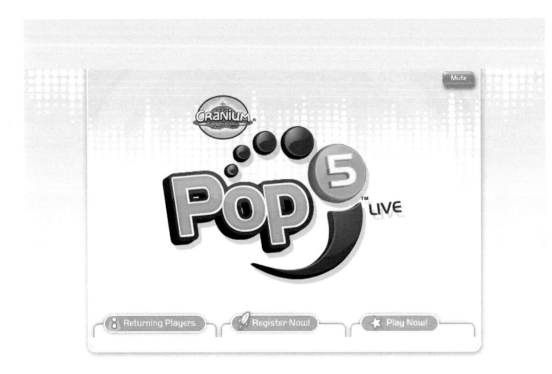

"How do you market an 'analog board
game' through digital means?
You create a viral gaming experience
where YouTube meets American Idol!"
BLITZ

The Brief

When Cranium introduced their newest board-game, POP 5, they wanted to create a digital game representation and site combo that would allow an online audience to experience the fun-natured party game in ways that would drive purchase intent. Beyond creating an engaging strategy, BLITZ was also faced with a technology challenge: to capture the core of the game, which is "it's not what you know, it's how you show it" – stressing that the experience of the board-game is much more about expressing your creativity via drawing, sculpting, humming, and acting. It was important that the game be perceived as entertainment for the masses, rather than simply the brainiacs.

The Challenge

How do you highlight the fun and excitement of a physical board-game online in a way that allows users to experience the thrill of participation and actual gameplay? How do you motivate people to not only play the game but engage them to submit their video performances? In addition to these strategy-based challenges, BLITZ also had some technological hurdles to get over. The site itself had to be live on two separate servers, be deployed on the MSN Games network, and allow users either to submit videos via Web capture or file upload – both of which had to be transcoded into Flash before running it through a hefty review process. Whew!

1 Million
games played

9 Minutes average
time played

28 Percent
conversion rate

The Solution

BLITZ translated the analog board-game into an online viral experience called "POP 5 Live", which allowed players throughout the country to challenge each other through video – it was like YouTube meets American Idol, with thousands of contestants competing for the chance to win a $50,000 cash prize by uploading videos. Visitors would play this online version just as if they were playing in a living-room with friends. Using the platform BLITZ built, players became performers in the game by creating and submitting new video content for other players to compete against. The game experience remained fresh as more content made its way in, so no game was ever the same twice. Performers were motivated to submit high-quality video, as their score was based on how many people guessed their clues correctly, and how well the video was rated. To gain initial traction, BLITZ seeded the game with hundreds of video performances by doing a three-day Hollywood shoot with comedic actors.

The Results

As the first-ever online game that was fully fueled by UGC, the campaign launch was a huge success, and became one of the prominent features on MSN Games for several weeks. It drew a huge fan-base and had an equally impressive conversion rate – 28% drove to purchase from all outgoing linkage. User-generated videos accounted for more than half the videos that were in rotation of the game, and average game-play was nine minutes. Cranium wished to achieve 500,000 game-plays, however, the game drew over 1,000,000. Another goal was for the game to get an official sponsor, which Alltel signed up for.

Safe for Work Viral – Diesel

"This is the best thing that has been made ever."
Kanye West

Client
Diesel

Credits
The Viral Factory
www.theviralfactory.com

Awards
D&AD, BTAA, Webby

www.break.com/index/
sfw-porn-clips.html

The Brief

Diesel was celebrating their thirtieth anniversary. To celebrate, Diesel were about to throw an incredible 24-hour global party extravaganza. Seventeen parties would take place during one day, kicking off in Tokyo, and continuing through seventeen countries across ten different time zones, concluding with a final climactic event in New York, 18 hours later.

Diesel would also be releasing a special "one day only", commemorative limited-edition, €30 model of jeans. While the jeans were limited to only 20,000 pairs worldwide, and over 50,000 of the public would be able to get tickets to the events, Diesel wanted to create a viral video to raise global awareness about the events, and reinforce its image as a bold, brave, iconoclastic lifestyle brand at this important milestone.

The Challenge

The challenge was to create a viral video that would drive as much visibility for the event and brand as possible. The solution would also need to work within Diesel's distinct brand values and new communications strategy. While not essential, the concept of the video should ideally relate to the "Dirty Thirty" and xXx concept, which described Diesel's "30th" anniversary in roman numerals, with an additional "adult & forbidden" meaning. To create a concept that would be "viral".

20 — Million video views

5,778 — Sites blogged

94 — Percent positive YouTube comments

The Solution

The concept twisted the "dirty thirty" aged and worn treatment concept into a far more warped and provocative meaning. The solution saw pornographic video scenes reconfigured with crude hand-drawn illustrations painted over the top of them. Turning cliché porn sequences into harmless scenes from a lively party, rendering them SFW, or "Safe For Work", the popular online term, after which the video is titled, used to distinguish what Web content can safely be viewed in the context of the work environment, and what might cost you your job! Other than the immediate shock realization that a major global brand had actually used real pornographic footage in an advertising campaign, much of the appeal is in deciphering the scenes, the muddled association of seeing childish acts being performed so erotically, and the comic solutions that were contrived to cover such explicit acts.

The Results

The video was stupendously controversial, and the perfect way of ensuring not only the viral spread of the video, but also as a way of increasing additional hype. Two weeks after launching and five days before the event, the video had received six million tracked views, with coverage on more than 600 sites, as well as being reported on TV. The video was instrumental in fuelling mass awareness about the xXx event, which was a sell-out many times over, and ensured queues hundreds long outside stores on the day the jeans were sold.

By October 15th, four days after the event, the total tracked views had reached almost 10 million, making it the most viewed viral of 2008. The total views by the first half of 2009 stood at over 20 million, and continues to remain relevant and deliver brand equity long after the event.

Qualitatively, the campaign provoked significantly more engagement with viewers than other virals, garnering thousands of comments, of which an outstanding 94% were positive from a randomly taken sample of YouTube comments. The audience was not solely viewers, but advocators forging a relationship between Diesel and the audience, way beyond the possibilities of other media.

The viral pushed the very limits of what is considered acceptable advertising, and puts Diesel at the forefront of exciting and edgy advertising, setting up Diesel as a brave brand willing to go down audacious routes but never diverging from their values.

In Search of the third Plush Poison

"The campaign result was excellent, and was able to translate wholesale the spirit that embraces the Plush Poison brand. That was definitely a key aspect in the success of the communication effort. The spontaneous media generated really came to our notice and we have only reasons to celebrate."
Danielle Medina, Tilibra

Client
Tilibra

Credits
W3haus
www.w3haus.com.br

www.plushpoison.com.br

The Brief

Tilibra, the biggest notebook company in Brazil, has a children's school stationery line named Plush Poison. The main characters from the Plush Poison line are two girls named Demi and Ivie. But these characters had almost no personality or biography. The only thing known about them is that they were into rock'n'roll. So, we were asked to create the brand's digital communication from scratch.

Sales were low and very few people were buying products from the Plush Poison brand. We turned to online tools such as Flickr and Orkut – Brazil's most popular social network – to find more information on the characters.

The Challenge

When searching for the Plush Poison characters on the Web, there were almost no results. Therefore, we had to create an online campaign that would put these characters on the map, appearing not only as a result on search platforms but also on social networks. To increase brand online awareness, increase sales, and get these characters close to their target were some of the goals that the interactive communication project should achieve.

To make that possible, the project had to be very easy to diffuse, using tools that would make it simple to pass on the campaign's information. The website's interface should also be as simple as possible. The campaign would then be a source of research regarding the brand's target, thus revealing the personalities and preferences of the Plush Poison girls.

04 Social Media

The Solution

To increase brand awareness and sales, we gave the girls personality and an online strategy to spread word about it. We identified the target's musical preferences and gave Demi and Ivie rock star personas. The campaign idea was the search for a third Plush Poison band member to join them. The creator of this third girl would be the winner.

To win the competition "In Search of the third Plush Poison", the user had to go through three phases: 1. Create an avatar to represent the third Plush Poison; 2. Be quizzed on their music knowledge; 3. Finally, win an online game that challenged their rhythm and time.

During the competition, site users could spread the word around the Internet, posting the campaign badge on their blogs. The badge with most hits would win the "best supporting crowd" prize.

The Results

The results were overwhelming: more than 35,000 avatars were created. Half a million votes were cast in 30 days. An astonishing ten minutes average stay was reached. Not to mention the thousands of avatars spontaneously posted on Flickr and other social tools. Vote casting became very popular on Orkut.

Even after the competition was over, its results were still a matter of discussion on several social networks. Participants kept on commenting on the look of the winning avatars. The story created for Demi and Ivie connected the brand with its public, resulting in user-generated media. It also assured an audience for future Plush Poison campaigns.

300,000
Site visits

10
Minutes average time

144,000
Unique users

35,000
Registrations

adidas Football Sign for your club

"This is the first chance I have of getting this close-up and cosy with my favourite player without physically being at a game. The personalised downloads from each player are right good and I cannot wait to show my friends."
Fan of Chelsea FC, Blog post

Client
adidas International Marketing BV

Credits
Neue Digitale/Razorfish
www.neue-digitale.de
blackbeltmonkey GbR
www.blackbeltmonkey.com

Awards
FWA, ADC, Eurobest

www.neue-digitale.de/projects_
adidas_football_website/

The Brief
The aim of the interactive campaign for five of the biggest and most successful football clubs in Europe, Chelsea FC, Liverpool FC, AC Milan, Real Madrid, and FC Bayern München is to increase the sale of shirts for the clubs. Thus, the websites should generate potential customer leads and forward them to the respective club's online store.

Furthermore, the site should strengthen the fan-team relationship and win new fans for the team. An additional goal is to intensify the team's connection with its fans. adidas would like to reach football fans around the world, especially fans of the featured teams as well as fans in Asia.

The Challenge
Many people claim that professional football players are inapproachable demigods – like superstars who can only be seen on TV. Therefore the five football clubs needed a way to get closer to their fans and thank them for their support. Since the target group is quite Internet savvy and most of the fans use their mobile phones heavily, the digital channel seemed to be the solution. To meet the fans' needs using the right tone, a strategy was developed to allow users to interact with the football stars, meet them up close and personal – in order to connect fans to the players and the clubs.

04 Social Media

The Solution

Thanks to interactive close-up video sequences fans get to spend a few minutes one-on-one with their favourite player: fans and users can demonstrate their loyalty for their respective football club by digitally signing a shirt belonging to their favourite football player. They then add their name and also upload a picture of themselves. The top four players from every club "personally" hand the user their custom shirt and officially welcome them to the club.

After signing the shirt it automatically lands in a "never-ending" gallery with all the other fan shirts. All participants automatically qualify to take part in the club's contest.

Users can also download a personal video of one of their stars – like Michael Ballack – to their mobile phone or integrate it in their own blog. Using the mobile screensaver, fans and users can always see which new shirts have been added to the site. Users are also forwarded to the respective club's online store and can order their own shirt. Additionally, the user receives access to information that ordinarily only official club members have, such as behind-the-scenes information, films, and player interviews.

Chelsea FC fans can also be part of the world's longest team photo with the players.

670,000
Page views

500,000
Unique visitors

96,617
Shirt signatures

73,851
Registrations

65,900
Mobile elements downloaded

The Results

The campaign's visually and technically complex implementation is also inviting to users who are not Chelsea FC fans and the website offers users personal and emotional interaction with their football heroes and their favourite football clubs.

The campaign was successfully accompanied by measures such as viral videos, banners, and LED big-screen advertising in stadiums in the team's country. Thanks to the seamless integration of the various components the online campaign broke registration and download records and became a benchmark for the participating top clubs in Europe.

Cravendale Join IN

"W+K London and unit9 have made a
really brilliant thing. It's part multi-player
interactive game/muckabout, part UGC,
part video editor..."
Iain Tait, crackunit.com

The Brief

Cravendale milk wanted to jolt viewers and give them a reason to sit up and take notice of milk once again. But behind the apparent mayhem, there was a point with the message, that this was not just any milk, but "filtered to make it purer."

The "Milk Matters" campaign spearheaded by a series of TV adverts from Wieden + Kennedy London featured, rather randomly, a pirate, a cow, and a cyclist involved in a series of hilarious escapades as they go to any lengths to get their hands on Cravendale. The website needed to expand on the success and creativity of the TV commercials, creating an online extension that would allow people to get involved, and bring the characters to life in a fun and interactive way.

The Challenge

The biggest challenge we faced was creating a website with video recording and editing functionality whilst keeping the experience completely intuitive and fun. Ultimately we wanted users to make their own film, but we didn't want this to be a barrier or have a steep learning curve. We needed the user to start having fun from the first click. So the user involvement needed to be simple, immediately rewarding, and progressive. In the first layer it's fun to wander around and try out the different moves, in the second layer one can challenge other characters to a dance-off, and in the third layer users can click the big red button and record anything. A wide shot, a close-up, discovering new functionality in a playful and engaging way.

04 Social Media

Client
Cravendale Milk

Credits
Wieden + Kennedy London
www.wklondon.com
unit9
www.unit9.com

Awards
FWA, One Show

www.unit9.com/archives/cravendale

The Solution
A multi-user game as the online extension of a TV commercial. Enter a name, choose a character and away you go. You are in the world of Cravendale. Join in, have fun. The site allows users to select any character depicted in the TV ads and create their own 60-second films. Users can collaborate, interact, and play together in a live environment. Viewers can share the movie-making experience with live visitors on the site, or can create a private set with their close friends. There are goodies hidden around the site – find them and you get IM icons, wallpapers, desktop icons, mobile wallpapers, and printable graphics for your T-shirt.

The Results
The spontaneous nature of the site has generated much attention from the online community. You never know what to expect or who you'll meet when you come to the site. The campaign has been a huge success story and traffic to the site has risen by 250% in the first 12 months.

Today Cravendale is the number one milk brand, with sales accounting for 3.7% of all milk bought in the UK and growing at 33% year-on-year. Following the marketing campaign, sales reached over £105 million, up from £80 million before the campaign.

250 Percent traffic increase

105 Million pounds in sales

99 Country visitors

61.6 Percent of users recording video

Häagen-Dazs Loves Honey Bees

"We're not only raising brand awareness
but making a difference in the world."
Katty Pien, Brand Director
for Häagen-Dazs

The Brief
Create an online space in support of the "Häagen-Dazs Loves Honey Bees" program, an initiative drawing attention to the growing crisis of the honey bee. The honey bee population has been decimated in recent years by an epidemic known as Colony Collapse Disorder (CCD). The "Häagen-Dazs Loves Honey Bees" initiative encourages the public to support the bees simply by eating ice cream, as a portion of the proceeds are directed to funding bee research programmes.

The goal for the helpthehoneybees.com website was to create a hub for consumers to learn more about Häagen-Dazs' commitment to saving the honey bees and to get involved with the cause.

The Challenge
To help visitors create an emotional attachment with the bees and inspire them, the website needed to be a rich and lush experience, and also fast to load. These two objectives are rarely achieved together. From a creative point of view we decided to approach this microsite as an opportunity for crafted design. We developed all the bee assets in 3-D in order to give them a realistic texture, consistent with the organic feel used by Häagen-Dazs: hand painting the clouds and fields, adding as many details as possible to make the interactive experience more rewarding.

From a technical point of view the challenge was to guarantee a smooth navigation in the rich bee field, containing the file size at the same time.

Client
Häagen-Dazs

Credits
Goodby, Silverstein & Partners
www.goodbysilverstein.com
unit9
www.unit9.com

Awards
FWA, One Show,
European Design Awards, .Net

www.unit9.com/helpthehoneybees

04 Social Media

Social Media
Häagen-Dazs Loves Honey Bees

193 ‒ Country visitors

6 ‒ Minutes average time on site

30 ‒ Dependent flavours

14,700 ‒ Google search results

The Results

Häagen-Dazs says it's seen sales increase 16% for the year. Brand advocacy for Häagen-Dazs among consumers hit 69%, the highest among 19 brands tracked. Every major media channel in America picked up on the story and helped champion the cause. Two weeks after the launch Häagen-Dazs reached 125 million page impressions, their goal for the entire year.

In June 2008, Häagen-Dazs and a coalition of beekeepers testified on the bees' behalf, in front of Senator Hillary Clinton and the House Agricultural Sub-Committee on Capitol Hill. In November 2008, Advertising Age honoured Häagen-Dazs as one of the Top 50 Brands of the Year.

The Solution

A bee guide follows your mouse as you explore a luxurious honey field and discover just how important bees are to us. Visit the "make your own bee" section. Have fun creating your very own little bee avatar to save to your desktop or send in a bee-mail to raise awareness. We added as many details as possible to make the interactive experience rich and rewarding. Idle states for the bee guide act out if you are idle, and animations, sounds, beautiful trees, and lush grass are all details that contribute to the quality of the site and the enjoyment of the experience itself.

Octavia RC

"The Octavia RC, the new KITT."
bligg.be

The Brief

Škoda introduced their renewed Octavia in the Netherlands. The tagline was "Improved on over 50 points". Critics said that the car had hardly changed, but the gist of the pay-off was it had changed in so many ways that it was hard to see it was still an Octavia. Škoda wanted an interactive campaign that would generate attention for the new model and would introduce it to the Netherlands.

The Challenge

We came up with the concept of the Octavia RC. RC stands for Remote Control. We asked the Dutch public to help us introduce the renewed Octavia. By giving website visitors live control over the car that would be parked in different locations in the Netherlands, they could see the live reaction of the passers-by. Obviously, controlling the car should be as easy as clicking the mouse, and the whole production of the two-week campaign period had to be carefully planned and produced.

Client
Škoda the Netherlands

Credits
Achtung!
www.achtung.nl

www.octaviarc.nl

The Solution

We customised a real Octavia and plugged it in to the Internet via UMTS on the laptops that were integrated in the car. The challenge consisted of building the car and allowing calls from the website to the car, which actually controlled the lights, played audio files, honked the horn, and activated the wipers, while different live video streams were sent back to the campaign site. These streams were visible to all the website visitors.

We wanted to use a seeding strategy to generate attention. It kicked off by adding a tab in the Octavia's product site that mentioned the Octavia RC.

When the campaign went live a test video of the car that was shot was posted on YouTube and went out to different blogs and e-zines. By thoroughly testing the car, the controls, and the connection we made sure nothing went wrong during the two-week action period.

130,000 Site visits

100 Blog posts

6 Minutes average time on site

60 People queuing

The Results

The Dutch automotive press started ringing Škoda when the Octavia RC tab appeared, and that started the discussion on fan forums. Blogs started writing about the car, and it was even mentioned in the leading Dutch national newspaper.

Over 100 international blogs were posted about the campaign, and people were wondering if it was real. An average of 60 people were almost constantly queuing to control the car and daily highlights were posted on the site.

In the two-week campaign period over 100,000 people visited the website, spending an average of six minutes on the site.

All in all, the campaign received a lot of positive attention and feedback.

Total Drama Island Interactive

"Total Drama Island is an example of a show that truly was immersive beyond linear television. It was the first animated reality show on television, and kids got caught up in the characters and went to TotalDramaIsland.com to follow up on the continuing stories and watch video beyond the linear show, and also to play games. We saw hits on TotalDramaIsland.com go up before, during, and after the show aired. There was a real connection back and forth between television and online."
Stuart Snyder, Turner Broadcasting

The Brief

Most teens think a trip to cottage country means hanging out with friends on the dock and soaking up the great outdoors – but they've never seen Total Drama Island! This animated reality series puts an unlikely group of teenagers together with one mission – survive the summer.

Total Drama Island is a 26-part animated TV and online series. A lampoon of reality TV, each week one of the contestants is voted off the island after enduring outrageous competitions, backstabbing gossip, and inedible summer-camp food. Dreams of celebrity lured them here, but these teens are in for a summer of romantic trysts and dark moments of betrayal.

Total Drama Island – Totally Interactive! transposes the drama of the show to an online game world that is updated and synchronised according to what's happening in the TV series on air that week.

The Challenge

In the earliest stages of development for Total Drama Island, production company Fresh TV approached Emmy Award-winning cross-platform studio Xenophile Media to create an online enhancement for the series that would keep viewers connected to the show in a meaningful way, generating buzz and excitement while promoting greater viewer numbers. In short, we needed to create a real cross-platform experience that would drive viewers from TV to online and back again.

For practical business reasons, we also needed to ensure that the enhancement would be seen as a valuable asset by TV broadcasters. Although designed to augment the TV series, the online property also needed to provide an additional source of distribution revenue.

04 Social Media

Client
TELETOON Canada

Credits
Xenophile Media, Inc.
www.xenophile.ca
Jam3Media
www.jam3media.com

Awards
International Emmy
Award Nomination

http://tdi.teleetoon.com

The Solution

The result was a deceptively simple proposal.

Each week, after watching the show on TV, viewers go online, create their own avatar and compete to play games based on the challenges in the TV series. At the end of the season, the top 22 players are then entered in a draw to win a walk-on role for their avatar in the final episode of the TV series.

And just for playing games, players earn "marshmallows" – an in-game currency which can then be redeemed to purchase avatar customisations and other online prizes. A weekly online tabloid featuring characters from the show along with the exploits of your own online camper is also distributed to players by email to keep them connected to the TV show and the online competition.

The main navigational interface depicts the island setting visually with all the 22 characters from TV, who are then voted off progressively as the series continues. The sense of "visiting the island" and competing with recognised characters reinforces the Total Drama Island brand, giving players the sensation that they are participating with the characters from the show.

The Results

Total Drama Island was an enormous hit during its initial premiere on Teletoon in Canada, with the online game world generating an unprecedented 70% conversion rate of TV viewers to registered players online.

The interactive property was then packaged with the TV series and distributed internationally where it has been sold to more than 30 countries in eleven languages.

Since its launch, Total Drama Island – Totally Interactive! has been a runaway success, boasting an accumulated fan-base of almost 5.5 million registered players around the world.

The success of Total Drama Island – Totally Interactive! demonstrates that the kids respond enthusiastically to interactive extensions of TV programming customised to their needs and interests. The property also earned an International Interactive Emmy Award nomination in 2008.

5.5
Million registered users

30
Countries playing

11
Different languages

70
Percent crossover from broadcast viewers to registered online players

Grêmio Star

"This campaign was unprecedented. No football team has bought or adopted a star before. Right now, some clubs are probably thinking: 'Why didn't I think about it before?' Well, too late. Grêmio is the first to name a star. Other clubs will have to run after theirs."
Rodrigo Rodrigues, User

The Brief

On December 11, 1983, Grêmio Football Porto Alegrense, the top Brazilian Team, won the Club World Championship, after beating Hamburger SV by 2-1 in Tokyo.

To celebrate the 25th year of this tournament, considered in Brazil the most important title a football club can win, Grêmio wanted something as big as the world. Although the budget was low, the expectations were high. The club wanted a campaign that could make Grêmio supporters not only remember that match, but also buy the retro 1983 shirt and the whole World Championship Anniversary product line. The challenge was to make the older supporters remember the match once more, and to make the younger ones become aware of the importance it had.

The Challenge

With few resources to build and spread an interactive campaign, it was impossible to create a sophisticated website, or to make a continuous seeding effort. Therefore, we had to create a fact that would feed the web platform, and spread around the media and influence supporters. Some rules needed to be observed. First of all, the campaign had to be understood by people of all ages, places, and social status, as the club's support-base is composed of millions of people all around the country. Then, all the content generated by the user had to be restricted and moderated, to avoid inappropriate rival supporters' responses.

04 Social Media

Client
Grêmio Football Porto Alegrense

Credits
W3haus
www.w3haus.com.br

www.estrelagremio.com.br

The Solution

The prestigious title has been represented for 25 years by a golden star embroidered on the club shirt. Inspired by this symbol we created something that reflected the greatness of the team's victory: the adoption of a real star, the "Grêmio Star". We gave the name Grêmio to a star in the sky, then made a hotsite announcing it. Accessing the hotsite, it was possible to see the star on Google Sky, watch the game's highlights and leave comments.

The project demanded a considerable effort in media coverage and public relations. A huge event to launch the campaign brought together the most important sports writers in the country. The comments written by site users appeared in the sky next to the Grêmio Star, composing an online constellation of Grêmio supporters.

The Results

The results were immediate: the unexpected adoption of the star led to spontaneous articles in all the major newspapers, on radio and TV in Brazil. Thousands of bloggers wrote about the campaign. Even other teams' supporters unwillingly helped just by commenting on the news.

Over 70,000 people visited the website, increasing the sales of commemorative merchandise of the Club World Championship, both on and offline. And for the first time in Grêmio's history an online campaign influenced and guided all offline advertising. During December, an off-season period in which there is almost no media on football, the attention was all drawn to Grêmio.

Grêmio Star was the subject of social media websites, and commented on by many Grêmio supporters, who even used the URL www.estrelagremio.com.br on their Orkut profiles.

86,503 — Visitors in December 2008

37,868 — Unique visitors

3,000 — Stars created

5 — Orkut communities created

Comcast Town

"Comcast Town – Interactive done right."
Youth Marketing

Client
Comcast

Credits
Goodby, Silverstein & Partners
www.goodbysilverstein.com
unit9
www.unit9.com
Nexus
www.nexusproductions.com

Awards
FWA

www.comcasttown.com

The Brief

Comcast, the US cable and high-speed Internet provider, is promoting its Triple Play package with an integrated advertising campaign that is optimistic and aspirational in tone, filled with dead-pan irony and semi-absurd humor.

Goodby, Silverstein & Partners of San Francisco invited unit9 to create the Comcast Town interactive experience. The goal was to offer website visitors the chance to experience the amazing world of the TV campaign, developed by Nexus Productions by creating an experience that goes beyond 30-second TV spots and targets an audience interested in visual and interactive innovation. Online users move into Comcast Town, design their ideal apartment, and enter a competition to win the grand prize of a real-world room remodel worth $30,000.

The Challenge

To create an interactive website that would allow you to fill a virtual living-room with pixel-based furniture, and expect discerning web surfers to participate, is a challenge in itself. The challenge we set ourselves was to get the audience to smile while playing this site.

Ultimately this is a concept that lives or dies by the "cool factor". The site needs to be captivating and allow users to register with minimal hassle. The sound effects, the hand-drawn icons, the adorable graphics, all combine to make a site that you just want to click around on. Comcast invited influential blogs within the digital set to design items of furniture that people could use and to form the jury to judge the best apartment in Comcast town.

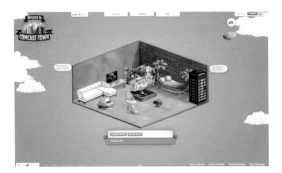

The Solution

Comcast Town, a website that mixes gaming, social networking, and engaging user interaction. Choose a neighborhood and then design your ideal Comcast crib. Fine-tune it and start to accrue currency using the capabilities of the Triple Play feature (TV, phone, Internet). Personalization is the key. We designed an interactive environment where users can select, buy, change layout, and make up their room as a reflection of themselves. Residents can add notes to each item they own and communicate with fellow residents via internal email and a guestbook functionality. This isn't a campaign which is consumed within a short period; this site will evolve with the players. The site uses Facebook Connect, enabling users to use their Facebook credentials to log in, keeping registration hassle to a minimum.

The Results

The website creates an experience that keeps visitors coming back and interacting with the brand by giving them the opportunity to earn currency every step of the way.

We worked closely with Facebook – partnering our application with theirs enables a more seamless experience for the end user and facilitates them sharing activities in Comcast Town with friends. At the core of this experience there is the new consumer who creates his or her own playground, own comfort zone, own universe. It's the empowered and better-informed and switched-on consumer.

The campaign is still in its infancy with a major feature update happening shortly. Results to date, 12/05/09, show 19,922 fully registered users with 6,536 log-in via Facebook Connect.

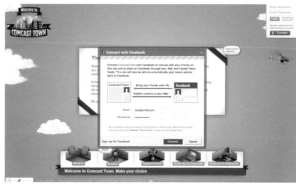

32.6 —
Percent signed
up via Facebook
Connect

20,000 —
Registered users

11.4 —
Percent users in the
design competition

4 —
Video Easter eggs

3 —
Game Easter eggs

FunkTube

"We understand that, because Brazilian Funk is a musical style from the fringes, FunkTube should be an authentic community, only counting on Som Livre for sponsorship, with no operational interference from the latter. FunkTube and the CD were a success."
Murilo Lico, Creative Director of SantaClaraNitro

The Brief

Som Livre is one of the most traditional recording labels in the country; it is part of GLOBO Organizations, the Brazilian media giant.

Som Livre has one of the largest record listings in the country and has always launched its recordings using a video clip of the artist singing parts of their songs. This work has always been done internally by the label's house agency.

The new market trends have made Som Livre rethink its communication strategies in a scenario characterised by the downward spiralling sales and the ever-increasing problem of piracy. Faced with these challenges, the label sought the help of an independent agency, thus coming to SantaClaraNitro.

The Challenge

Our challenge was to launch a music CD of Brazilian funk, "Pancadão do Caldeirão", a product with a young and very popular appeal. But this project ran into its own peculiar challenge: Brazilian funk is popular among the lower-income bracket, which is in turn the biggest consumer of pirated material in the country and used to dealing in bootleg music in MP3 format. Adding to this, funds for the FunkTube project were extremely limited, around US$40,000.

Client
Som Livre Records

Credits
SantaClaraNitro
www.santaclaranitro.com
DS|One
www.dsone.com.br
A Bendita
www.abendita.com

Awards
El Ojo de Iberoamerica, Cannes,
Grande Prêmio de Mídia do Estadão,
Melhor do Rio, Sinos

http://www.youtube.com/
watch?v=yecp97Bd8_U

04 Social Media

The Solution

To generate interaction between the consumer and the product through the creation of a Brazilian funk choreography competition. TV spots encouraged the public to record their own performance and send them to the website, where they could also watch and vote for the best video. Consumers shared videos through Orkut (Brazilian Facebook), blogs, YouTube, and other virtual communities, in order to get votes. The person with the most popular video would get his or her 15 minutes of fame in a live performance on a popular network TV programme.

The Results

FunkTube and the CD were a success.

It became an authentic brand community with a life of its own: within three months the website had more than 10 million hits, the videos sent by the users – more than 2,900 – were seen 3.8 million times and almost 1 million votes were counted.

Google registered 3,900 references to FunkTube, even some originating from outside Brazil. Some of the participants even had fan clubs set up on the net. The live TV programme featuring the winners was seen by about 12 million people.

The community set up around Brazilian funk became a brand valued by Som Livre at more than US$1.2 million.

The CD went platinum and exceeded its sales objectives by 250%.

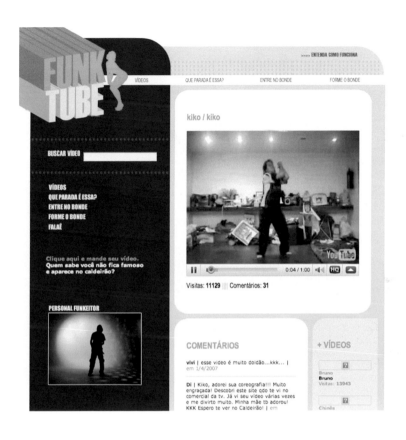

kiko / kiko

Visitas: **11129** ||| Comentários: **31**

COMENTÁRIOS

vivi | esse vídeo é muito doidão...kkk... |
em 1/4/2007

Di | Kiko, adorei sua coreografia!!! Muito
engraçada! Descobri este site qdo te vi no
comercial da tv. Já vi seu vídeo várias vezes
e me divirto muito. Minha mãe tb adorou!
KKK Espero te ver no Caldeirão! | em

+ VÍDEOS

Bruno
Bruno
Visitas: 13943

Chinês

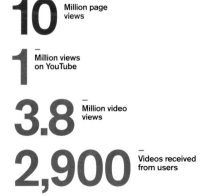

10 — Million page
views

1 — Million views
on YouTube

3.8 — Million video
views

2,900 — Videos received
from users

Eternal Moonwalk –
A tribute to Michael Jackson

"A plethora of blogs have popped up over
the past week memorializing Michael
Jackson. However, when it comes to the
moonwalk, this is the best one we've
seen yet: The Eternal Moonwalk."
Faith-Ann Young, justintimberlake.com

Client
Studio Brussel

Credits
group94
www.group94.com
mortierbrigade
www.mortierbrigade.com

Awards
FWA

www.eternalmoonwalk.com

The Brief
After the shocking news of Michael Jackson's death, an idea was born. The idea was simple: create a viral tribute site sponsored by a radio station. In doing so the goal was to raise awareness of the Flemish radio station Studio Brussel, whilst also paying tribute and allowing users to leave their mark of respect for one of the icons of the entertainment industry.

The Challenge
The true challenge was to translate this simple idea into an engaging Web experience within the shortest time-frame possible. Starting from scratch, there wasn't even a domain name, it took the group94 team no more than three days (and nights) before we could put this project live, including content management, databases, video upload, community tools, statistics...

04 Social Media

The Solution
The site centers around the famous moonwalk. Starting off with Michael Jackson himself, it shows a never-ending video chain with user-generated moonwalks. Visitors are invited to film their own moonwalk, submit it to the website, and become part of the chain. For viral purposes each video can be accessed directly (via a unique URL) and there are very easy-to-use social-promotion tools to hand to this end.

The Results
The site immediately became a global success with over half a million visits three days after launch. It has been the most popular topic on Twitter for three consecutive days. Thousands of bloggers have been talking about the moonwalk, whilst Britney Spears and Justin Timberlake posted the site on their homepages. Also, all major traditional news channels have been picking it up, and it has been on several TV stations, including the BBC and CNN.

2 — Million unique visitors
(within 10 days)

9,000 — Moonwalks
submitted

200 — Submitting
countries

10 — Kilometers
moonwalk length

60 — TB bandwidth
used

Greenpeace (Special Feature)

Greenpeace Brazil on the Internet
The Internet is the central point of all of Greenpeace's campaigns. It's to the Internet that all the people who are touched by the messages turn for deeper information on each subject, or to participate in any cause.

Greenpeace Brazil believes that communicating the campaigns using creative ideas on the Internet is another positive feature this medium offers. That's because innovative presentation attracts intelligent users and potential activists, and also because this material can provide the best type of campaign: mouth-to-mouth. Or, in this case, msn-to-msn, email-to-email, blog-to-blog, Twitter-to-Twitter, etc.

Greenpeace uses the Internet to inform, reveal, and as a powerful tool to mobilise people. Online petitions are available for asking the government about its attitudes towards Amazon Rainforest deforestation and other critical issues. Greenpeace knows well how to use online media, and we can also say that Greenpeace uses it on behalf of the planet.

1. Transgenics

"This video explains in a clear way the dangers of transgenic food. It's an outrage that the government does not let us know what we are consuming."
Magnolia Matos Pereira,
Greenpeace's cyber activist

The Brief
Greenpeace Brazil needed to get signatures for a petition to be sent to the government, protesting against the approval of transgenic soya bean seeds and against this industry's monopoly.

The Challenge
Besides asking cyber activists to engage in support of the cause, Greenpeace also needed to convey the dangers of transgenic food for people and the environment.

The Solution
To clarify the "transgenic" subject in the minds of Brazilians, Greenpeace made a sort of cartoon documentary. In it, the announcer openly attacks the government, which is facilitating the formation of a monopoly in the production of transgenic soya bean seeds and contributing to the destruction of the planet's biodiversity.

The Results
This video promoted an increase of 20% in new contributors for Greenpeace. And what's more, the video was viralised via email.

Client
Greenpeace

Credits
AlmapBBDO
www.almapbbdo.com.br

www.youtube.com/
watch?v=mqYqwT6KRZM

34
Percent increase
in contributors
to Greenpeace Brazil

25,000
More people in
cyber activity

26
Percent
Greenpeace Brazil
website increase

2. Amazon Rainforest

The Brief
Greenpeace Brazil needed to show
the absurdly high rates of deforestation
during President Lula's term in office.

The Challenge
We needed to shock the population who
had no access to deforestation figures
and show by means of comparison the
size of the area that had been deforested.

The Solution
This video was developed to show the
ridiculous scale of deforestation, talking
about the calamity as if it was a real-
estate project. A spoof to shock the
users and a call for help.

The Results
This video promoted an increase of 20%
in new contributors for Greenpeace.
The video was viralised via email.

"Very well executed and with a
brilliant idea: explain with visual
examples the size of deforestation
in a cool and cynical visual language."
Sergio Abranches,
Brazilian journalist

Client
Greenpeace

Credits
AlmapBBDO
www.almapbbdo.com.br

Awards
FIAP Gold Medal

www.youtube.com/
watch?v=eb35cKLySo4

26 — Percent increase
in contributors
to Greenpeace Brazil

18,000 — More people in
cyber activity

20 — Percent
Greenpeace Brazil
website increase

3. Resta Um

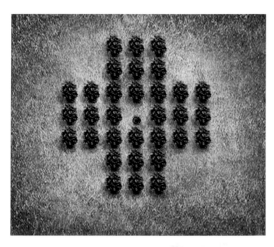

"An amazing ideal. A very smart way of showing how humans can be so stupid."
Internet user

The Brief
Greenpeace Brazil needed to show the absurdly high rates of deforestation during President Lula's term in office.

The Challenge
Show that 3,700,000 trees were being cut down per day, and also show the IQ of those who do nothing to stop it.

The Solution
A mobile game that resembled the famous Single Noble. But in place of the traditional pegs we had trees, and the more intelligent the player, the greater the damage to the forest.

An alert for the population about the dangers of human interference in nature, which has led to the extinction of important species and is the main cause of climatic changes in Brazil.

The Results
The game was downloaded from the site by thousands of users.

04 Social Media

Client
Greenpeace

Credits
AlmapBBDO
www.almapbbdo.com.br

Awards
One Show, D&AD, FIAP,
El Ojo de Iberoamerica, CCSP

http://200.186.92.250/awards/2007/
greenpeace/resta_touch/port/
arq/02.html

7.34 Percent rate of rich media

65,000 Mobile game downloads

1:09 Minutes average time on site

4. Scientist

The Brief
Show the impact of global warming in Brazil and in the rest of the world.

The Challenge
Show how climatic changes are much closer to the user who still believes they will only occur in 100 years' time.

The Solution
A digital experience that explains step-by-step to users the consequences of climatic changes. To participate, the user uploads a photo or uses the webcam to see his or her face in situations that symbolise climatic changes. At the end of the experience, the photo of the user's face is damaged to show how they are going to feel the consequences of global warming on their own skin.

The Results
Thousands of users participated in the site. The experience was so successful that Greenpeace International decided to adopt it in several countries around the world, serving as a flagship of its campaign against global warming.

"Perfect execution, brilliant idea and a slap in the face for those who still think global warming is a distant issue."
Joanna Guinle, Managing Director of Greenpeace Brazil

255,000 — Page views

185,000 — Unique users

Client
Greenpeace

Credits
AlmapBBDO
www.almapbbdo.com.br

Awards
Cannes, D&AD, FIAP, El Sol, El Ojo de Iberoamerica, LIA

http://200.186.92.250/awards/2007/greenpeace/cientista/port/

5. GreenTube

The Brief
Show the impact of global warming in Brazil and in the rest of the world.

The Challenge
Show how climatic changes are much closer to the user who still believes they will only occur in 100 years' time.

The Solution
A series of small videos on YouTube were created to alert people to the consequences of global warming. When users press play, they see in a straightforward way what is happening with the weather in the planet and how it is affecting the environment.

The Results
In less than two weeks, the videos had been discussed in more than 50 blogs around the world.

"Extremely creative and simple. These are the best ideas."
Internet user, Twitter.com

Client
Greenpeace

Credits
AlmapBBDO
www.almapbbdo.com.br

www.youtube.com/
watch?v=AKLcUbvCxHw

04 Social Media

80,000
— Unique visitors in the first month

15,788
— Blog posts

7.34
— Percent rate of rich media

6. WeAtheR

"Numerous sites are created for good
causes, and many of them send an
important message, yet lack creativity
and high-quality design and development.
This multiplayer strategy game is one
of the best examples I have seen of a
creative site with an important message."
Rob Ford, FWA (for Adobe Edge)

Client
Greenpeace

Credits
AlmapBBDO
www.almapbbdo.com.br

Awards
FWA, Cannes, FIAP, LIA,
One Show, D&AD, Wave Festival,
El Ojo de Iberoamerica, CCSP

www.greenpeaceweather.com.br

The Brief

Greenpeace WeAtheR was inspired by board-games, but unlike the game WAR players don't fight to conquer the world on their own; by using cooperation strategies they fight together to save the planet from climatic changes.

It is a multiplayer game. As soon as someone enters one of the game rooms the player becomes a Greenpeace activist. Their mission is to get together with the other players in a search for solutions to solve the environmental crisis that is affecting our planet.

The Challenge

All players have to fight against climatic changes and reverse crisis situations. To do so they can use action points, cards that they buy and discard, recruitment of new activists, air transport, and other manoeuvres. They agree on the rules of the game in a chat room. Emerging problems can arise in territories and if they're not solved in that specific round, they become bigger and more chronic.

The Solution

Our planet is suffering from disorganised development and is threatened by pollution and deforestation. Its future depends on non-governmental organisations, like Greenpeace, defending the environment from human aggression.

Despite being a subject that is much in vogue all over the world, global warming is still treated like a distant problem in Brazil, which is the world's fourth-largest emitter of pollutant gases. This situation is mainly the consequence of deforestation and slash and burn. In order for the population to demand that the government takes the necessary measures people need to join forces.

The game was developed in Brazil to try and attack this problem head on, by mobilising the young people who are going to inherit the consequences of climatic changes. But, in fact, this is a worldwide issue, so much so that Greenpeace WeAtheR has players all over the world in surprisingly large numbers.

The Results

Currently, the advergame is the most incisive way of making digital content more interactive, appealing and relevant.

In addition to creating and uniting a truly multiracial community behind a cause, WeAtheR has been generating lots of repercussions in blogs, having been mentioned in more than 7,800 posts. It was chosen as "site of the day" by FWA, one of the most important world-design thermometers and won a Lion at the 2008 Cannes Festival in the "gaming" category.

113,516 — Site visits

2 — Million page views

7:26 — Minutes average time on site

Since it went live it has spread like wildfire, without any publicity or specific campaign. In less than two months the game has been accessed in more than 136 countries. According to Google Analytics, there have been more than 1 million page views in this period.

Access ranking by country:
1. Brazil
2. USA
3. China
4. Germany
5. France

Outside the Web

In addition to being a multiplayer online game, Greenpeace WeAtheR also comes in a real-life version. Made from recycled wood and paper, the game can be bought on the site itself. Greenpeace is looking for partners to become involved in the production of the board-game. The major objective is to distribute the game to public schools in Brazil, which are lacking in quality teaching.

Corporate

Introduction by
Grégoire Assemat-Tessandier, Bacardi

05

orporate

Writing this introduction made me think about the meaning of Corporate and what I would expect to read. Corporate, in our global collective memory, goes way beyond its Latin origin, *corpus*, a body or body of people – read: suits, tie, grey carpet, cubicles, and that's just the thought starters.

Given that this is a book about where the Web meets Marketing meets Creativity, I will stick to what I know best and is, no doubt, the most fascinating combination of the corporate world: Brands and Digital.

"Brands are completely embedded in our lives, in our shared and personal memories. Some brands are not even brands any more: Xerox this? Hoover that! Got a Kleenex?"

Brands are completely embedded in our lives, in our shared and personal memories. Some brands are not even brands any more: Xerox this? Hoover that! Got a Kleenex? By nature, brands are the ultimate competitive machines. When unleashed in the consumer world, they have but one mission, to conquer, and we have developed many techniques to meet that objective: TV ads, media, PR, promotions, exclusivity, direct mail, CRM, discount, limited editions, research, innovation… All very powerful enablers to beat the competition, wherever it needs to be beaten: store shelves, shopping streets, consumers' minds, hearts or homes.

This world was well organised: brands had an ever-expanding list of competitors, using more or less identical techniques, each one gaining or losing market shares over time. A beautiful and never-ending sprint. And then, it happened, the Internet. After the first few exciting years of recruiting new talents, new agencies, and testing new ways to connect brands with consumers, it became apparent that it was a game-changer.

Two simple core factors made it very different: Always On & Technology. The first one is so overt that I probably should not even mention it. Nevertheless, its obvious nature is proportional to its impact on brands and corporations and thus should not be disregarded. For the first time, brands are connected to their consumers 24/7. Some might even argue that they are totally exposed, revealed or uncovered. And not just to their consumers, but also to rejecters, advocates, influencers, kids, mums, you name it! This has forced brands to adapt and develop Web platforms that are up to date, fresh, and kept relevant all year round.

This adaptation curve was steep as it required structural changes and original strategies that could only be developed by individuals or agencies with new and different skill sets. To make matters worse, this "always on" media allows consumers to access… well, pretty much anything. The battle for consumers' share of time, a very rare commodity these days, is on. And it's everyone against everyone.

"The second challenge with the Web is that it's intricately linked with the most violent stream of progress mankind has ever known: technology."

The second challenge with the Web is that it's intricately linked with the most violent stream of progress mankind has ever known: technology. Well, when you think about it, the Web is technology. And it never stops evolving. A one-year-old technical infrastructure is now obsolete and obviously needs to be updated. A cool and immersive Flash-based brand website is now old-fashioned and irrelevant.

Apologies, as this is where the "buzz-word roll" starts: cloud, semantic web, RFID, geo localisation, re-marketing, pre-marketing, APIs, etc… And here comes the bandwagon of user-generated content (videos, comments, ratings, reviews, feeds…), followed by social tools (social networks, micro-blogging, bookmarking aggregators…). Not one day passes without the same question: Which ones should be integrated in our brand digital platforms? How do we do it? Can we manage it? These questions are even more relevant now that the majority of these "buzz words" are completely assimilated into the consumer's life.

Here lies a fascinating dynamic: technology in a perpetual flux of evolution and brand Web platforms with a need to stay relevant but struggling to even keep up. A Web platform that cannot adapt within the right timeframe is the sign of a brand and a corporation that is becoming irrelevant, out of touch and out of sync with the competitive market. Clearly a sign of an endangered brand.

05 Corporate

Last year, some interesting evolution happened: skittles.com going full social, nike.com taking a blog-like structure and Red Bull connecting with Facebook.

Encouragingly this is just skimming the surface of the true integration of these amazing differentiating digital opportunities. And why not, in a not so far away future, brands going for a framework-less digital footprint? Or brands opting for fragmenting their digital presence, designing branded content for streams and directly embedding it within a variety of their consumer social contexts: branded videos on Vimeo or YouTube, events pictures on Flickr, consumer database in Facebook (the new CRM environment), Twitter as the new "one too many" communication (micro-blogging replacing newsletters).

Effectively, the famous, powerful .com becomes a directory for branded streams. So, which brand will be the first to challenge the king, the sacred .com? The seed might already be in the following pages…

Grégoire Assemat-Tessandier
Bacardi

Bio.
<u>Grégoire Assemat-Tessandier</u>
Bacardi

Grégoire Assemat-Tessandier
started a career in corporate
and business law. He quickly
switched to digital advertising,
and joined Publicis in Paris as
a copywriter. He evolved to
strategist, and was promoted
to Account Director. Worked
on international brands like
Garnier, Coca-Cola, Nestlé,
Diesel, amongst others.
Swam to London. Landed at
Lean Mean Fighting Machine
as Account Director. Worked
on Emirates Airlines, Coty
Prestige, Harper Collins, Canon.
Jumped client side to Bacardi
Global Brands as Global Digital
Marketing Manager.

Currently Global Head of
Digital – Bacardi Global Brands
–
www.bacardi.com

"So, which brand will
be the first one to
challenge the king,
the sacred .com?"

05 Corporate

Bacardi.com

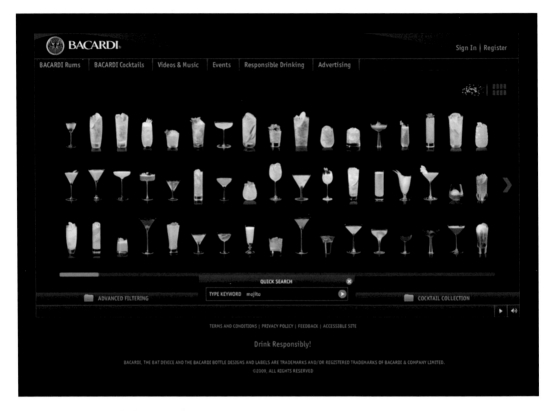

"Bacardi.com exhibits both form
and function, consistency and
flexibility – the perfect blend
for this modern heritage brand."
Betsy DiCarlo, Executive Vice
President, AgencyNet

The Brief

Bacardi's early and committed adoption of online marketing came with success and recognition, but it also brought with it the growing pains commonly faced by leaders and innovators. The Bacardi brand gradually became disjointed as a result of the decentralized efforts of their local markets. As the visual identity of the brand became increasingly diluted, its intrinsic values became lost on the consumer. AgencyNet was tasked with creating a global brand portal to provide a globally consistent infrastructure that would support local market efforts and maintain flexibility to accommodate specific local content.

The Challenge

The portal would need to be a powerful, rich, immersive experience, yet still SEO and Accessible-friendly. It would also require a robust global dashboard and content management system with multi-language capabilities as ease of implementation and speed of initiative deployment were also critical to its adoption by the local markets. The need for consistency globally with market flexibility, as well as capitalizing on economies of scale, were paramount in the portal strategy and build.

Client
Bacardi Global Brands

Credits
AgencyNet
www.agencynet.com

www.bacardi.com

The Solution
AgencyNet developed a robust global content infrastructure wrapped in an engaging, immersive digital experience. The homepage boasts full-screen edge-to-edge globally consistent videos that serve as a backdrop to local market content touts. The dynamic touts can be dragged vertically or hidden/revealed, allowing the user to be in control of the experience and to fully appreciate the video playing in the background or engage with the site's content. Behind the scenes, a series of Application Programming Interfaces (APIs), development kits, and a custom global dashboard housing a content management system were developed to aid local markets in the creation of their content.

The Results
This brand portal ultimately reduced the need for centralized, internationally-generic content and thus allowed local markets to engage their consumers with the familiar cultural nuances to which they respond. Most significantly, AgencyNet consolidated hundreds of scattered initiatives into a single, powerful, global portal for 27 countries and 20 different languages, giving Bacardi the platform they need for consistent, impactful and engaging digital advertising.

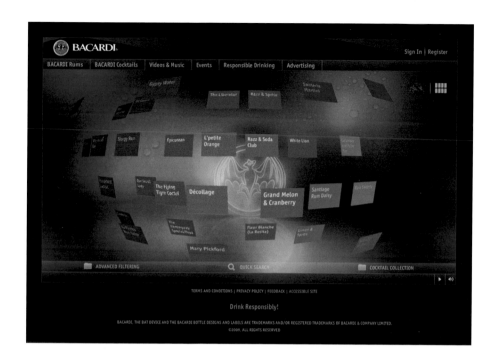

4 Million unique users

707,000 Google results

80,000 Registrations

20 Languages

27 Country markets

Road Runner

"This new generation of Road Runner is really a reinvention of what a broadband service should be."
Jeff King, Executive Vice President, Time Warner Cable Network Services and President, Road Runner

The Brief
Renowned American national cable company Time Warner Cable set out to rebuild the portal for their high-speed Internet brand Road Runner (RR), and contacted Fi for the latest design and technology guidance. The new site required a new and improved user experience, providing customers with the ability to take full advantage of broadband content and increasing Internet speeds. There was a desire to customize the RR Web experience to suit visitors' personal preferences.

The Challenge
Designing and reconstructing a complete portal, working with everything from system architecture to interactive design and 3-D graphics, with the overall objective of massively increasing revenue, was a major challenge. The site showcased a huge amount of content and several advanced rich media applications. Fi decided to produce the entire portal in Flash, a groundbreaking effort and phenomenal challenge at the time.

Client
Road Runner, Time Warner Cable

Credits
Fi
www.f-i.com

Awards
FWA, Flash Forward

www.rr.com

The Solution

By producing the RR site in Flash, we were able to capture a fluid and seamless experience that made the most of all the possibilities with a broadband connection. The site became dynamic, and a rich and engaging user experience. The style was a mixture of the RR visual brand in the form of the speedy Road Runner Loony Tunes cartoon character, but also a more mature and serious side to show that RR was one of the biggest players in the portals of the Web. RR.com was ahead of its time, in that it took the concept of aggregating everything a user required in one place, and tying it together under the brand of a premium paid service provider.

The Results

Awarded with FWA Site of the Year, winner of the Flash Forward Film Festival Award for Technical Merit, increased yearly revenue from 800k to 90m and spoken about in tons of magazines – Road Runner was a true success! Ultimately, but providing more of what the user wants (email, weather, games, TV listings) in one place, and introducing Google into a portal (the first such implementation), the site was a success.

When only two years old, Fi and Road Runner decided it was time to take the next step. The portal was rebuilt, making it even better. The loading times, speed, and performance were greatly improved as well as adding new and valuable extra features.

RR.com has been, and continues to be, one of the most talked about Flash websites ever built.

90

Million U.S. dollars per year revenue – increase from $867,000

3.9

Minutes average time on site

4

Million Google results

Got Milk?

"gotmilk.com was way overdue for a makeover, and that required an artistic sensibility and a sense of humor to match the iconic brand's enviable place in pop culture. It needed to be fun, interactive and informative. Check. Check. Check."
Steve James, Executive Director, California Milk Processor Board

Client
The California Milk Processor Board

Credits
Goodby, Silverstein & Partners
www.goodbysilverstein.com
unit9
www.unit9.com

Awards
FWA, Cannes, One Show, New York Festivals

www.gotmilk.com

The Brief

For 15 years, the goal of the "got milk?" campaign has been to take milk, a pretty traditional commodity, and make it feel interesting, important, and valuable. The advertising worked well over the years to do this. The brand website, gotmilk.com, did not, alas. It was built in the earlier days of the "information superhighway" and never kept up with the times. Rather, it was a static, hard-to-navigate clearing house for a bunch of information. The California Milk Processor Board asked us to re-imagine, redesign, and re-launch the site so that it would live up to the brand and communicate our strategy.

The Challenge

The "got milk?" brand strategy has been to position milk as a super-drink because it offers a host of health benefits – help with healthy hair, nails, skin, strong teeth, bones, and muscles, sleep, and even symptoms of PMS. Although it was necessary for the new site to house a wealth of content, like pro-milk medical studies and milk-based recipes, it first and foremost needed to quickly and memorably deliver the super-drink message to anyone stopping by. The challenge: how to do a lot of informational heavy lifting in such a fun, engaging way that people scarcely realize they're being stuffed full of health facts and reasons to drink more milk?

Corporate
Got Milk?

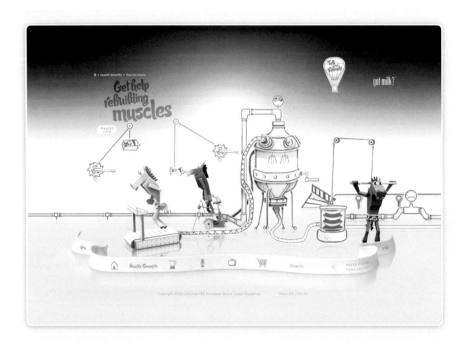

850,000
Site visits

3:48
Minutes average
time on site

4.6
Million page
views

1,025
Blog posts

The Solution

Imagine discovering the place where all the best performance drinks are created and packaged. A magical, complicated contraption packages an elixir that promotes healthy hair, one that helps with muscle rebuilding, and even a drink that reduces the symptoms of PMS. Now imagine that each container is being filled with the same amazing liquid: milk.

Inspired by milk cartons, the intricate machine appears to be constructed entirely of paper. Even the animals that run the operation are 3-D paper models. Through a series of games, these quirky characters teach users more about what makes milk a super-drink. Winners unlock a downloadable pattern to create a paper character of their own.

The Results

Within two months of launching the revamped gotmilk.com, monthly traffic doubled. Visitors spent an average of nearly four minutes on the site, a 140% increase over the average time spent on the old site. People played the games – they were successful in drawing people in – but they also spent time reading background information on milk's benefits and looking through milk smoothie recipes. The site has outperformed the Google Analytics Gaming index on time spent (by a minute) and user interactions (by 60%). And the California Milk Processor Board believes they finally have a site that delivers their message, engages Californians, and is a true reflection of the "got milk?" brand.

Metro.lu

01 About Metro   02 Advertisers   03 Investors

About Metro   The Paper   The Market   The Reader   Metro Life Panel   Contact Us

Case Studies   Brand Extensions   Previous Advertisers   Metro Formats   Beyond the Paper   Creative Specifications

360° of news
Metro: around the world

Case studies

Sex And The City

Air Berlin

National Treasure. Book of Secrets.

HP

Sex And The City

Metro is the perfect vehicle for advertisers to reach their audiences. Many of the world's leading brands are already using Metro as an effective answer to their marketing needs.

Brief

New Line Cinema knew that following on from the phenomenal success of the Sex & The City movie, millions of women would want to take home the exploits of Carrie, Samantha, Charlotte and Miranda on celluloid or rather DVD as soon as it hit stores. The question was, how were they going to make young, urban, professional women, just like the Sex & The City girls, aware of the imminent release of the DVD and do this in the most memorable way?

"We're delighted with metro.lu – it represents our global, urban brand values in a professional and attractive way. And it's easy for us to use, which means we're able to have the most up-to-date information available for our partners & customers to use."
Sidonie Kingsmill, Metro,
Global Marketing Director

The Brief

Metro International, publisher of Metro, the world's fourth-largest newspaper by readership, needed to redevelop their corporate website – to attract advertisers and investors with all the real-time information they require to consider Metro International as a valued partner.

The Challenge

unit9 created a solution that gives Metro total control over all aspects of the website content. Now Metro's global marketing team is able to quickly and simply keep the information accurate and relevant. All content is edited online, down to the copy in the Flash banners, animations, interactive map, and case studies. The solution required the integration of Flash with external services for financial data, and a bespoke CMS solution designed to integrate with the existing Metro workflow.

Client
Metro

Credits
Metro
www.metro.lu
unit9
www.unit9.com

www.metro.lu

-WORLD'S LARGEST INTERNATIONAL NEWSPAPER-

-WORLD'S LARGEST INTERNATIONAL NEWSPAPER-

The Solution

unit9 conceived a website that not only appeals to the Metro global readership but serves as a sophisticated marketing tool aimed at investors and advertisers, providing immediate access to Metro's market insights, reader profiles, and global distribution system.

Inspiring animations accompany the visitor journey, revealing bite-sized market insights inviting further exploration. This data is constantly changing. The relevancy and accuracy of the global distribution and readership is key to the Metro marketing strategy.

To further assist the Metro global sales team, the interactive map, "360° of news", able to display Metro's international local presence and link through to advertising case-studies, can be downloaded to run offline as an always-updated rich media presentation tool.

The Results

The website has allowed Metro to gain credibility with its primary target of investors and advertisers and provides better support for the sales team on the ground.

The website now acts as a tool to help clients and agencies plan their local and global campaign by accessing real-time stats on readership demographics and key facts.

360° of news
Metro: around the world

Advertising
showcase

Award winning
creative in action

Europe's most read
newspaper with over

23.1 million

daily readers

01 About Metro   02 Advertisers   03 Investors

About Metro   The Paper   The Market   The Reader   Metro Life Panel   Contact Us

Jump to
▶ Young
▶ Active and Career Minded
▶ Modern Consumers
▶ Early Adopters and Tech Savvy
▶ Curious About the World
▶ Working Hard, Playing Hard

Our Readers
The definition of a Metro reader

What type of person reads Metro? The type of person who usually doesn't have the time to read papers!

Metro readers are busy; they have demanding careers and eventful social lives. Typically in their early thirties, they are well educated, well paid metropolitan professionals. From career choices and holiday adventures, to cars, property and fashion labels, Metro readers know exactly what they want and have the means to get it. Male or female, they are enthusiastic socialites, making the most of their free time and the city they live in. They are heavy internet users, shop online and love technology and gadgets. So, how does Metro target these cash rich but time poor people? Simple - we offer them the right news in the right place at the right time. By making Metro free and placing it in high traffic commuter zones, readers can pick up a copy every morning on their way to work without queues, hold-ups or hassle. Metro's unbiased views and strong mix of news and entertainment make it the perfect read during what is often the only downtime they enjoy in their working day, the morning commute. Obvious, when you think about it.

Young

Metro is a young paper attracting a young audience. Because 4 in 10 Metro readers are likely to be aged 18-35, a ratio over 30% higher than that of traditional press, Metro is better positioned to communicate with the younger target groups.

Age Profile of Readers   Traditional Press Readers - ▇

150 + Cities

360° of news
Metro: around the world

Advertising
showcase

Award winning
creative in action

01 About Metro   02 Advertisers   03 Investors

About Metro   The Paper   The Market   The Reader   Metro Life Panel   Contact Us

Jump to
▶ Young
▶ Active and Career Minded
▶ Modern Consumers
▶ Early Adopters and Tech Savvy
▶ Curious About the World
▶ Working Hard, Playing Hard

Our Readers
The definition of a Metro reader

What type of person reads Metro? The type of person who usually doesn't have the time to read papers!

Metro readers are busy; they have demanding careers and eventful social lives. Typically in their early thirties, they are well educated, well paid metropolitan professionals. From career choices and holiday adventures, to cars, property and fashion labels, Metro readers know exactly what they want and have the means to get it. Male or female, they are enthusiastic socialites, making the most of their free time and the city they live in. They

1 Guinness World Record: world's largest international newspaper

21 Million daily readers

15 Languages

56 Editions

recom

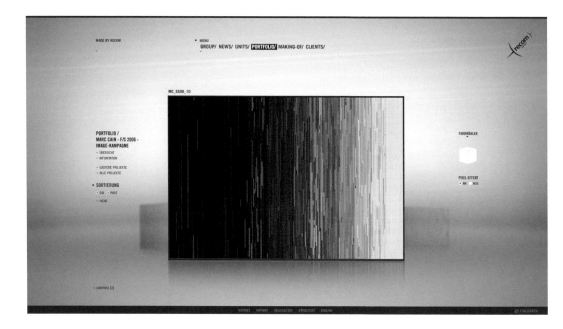

"Our new website shows, in a very dynamic way, the quality of the images produced by recom. Many clients have given us extremely positive feedback and statistics increased enormously. So finally our goal – to have a high-end presentation of our high-end work – is absolutely reached."
Lars Wittmaak, Management
recom GmbH

The Brief

Recom is one of the most renowned European studios for artwork, post production, and CGI. The relaunch was intended to reflect recom's growth and to give each of their three units, recom POST, recom CGI, and recom ART, a profile of its own.

Among other features, all the pictures of the recom POST and recom CGI portfolio database should be viewable in medium size or full screen without the browser elements. Visitors should also be able to put together a portfolio with an integrated "lightbox" function, export content by single download, zip-file as well as portfolio-PDF, to gather all information about a project.

The Challenge

The relaunch pursues two main goals: firstly, to provide a highly functional, easy-to-use tool for recom's professional visitors; secondly, to integrate recom's mission statement, "We put every pixel in the right spot", visually and functionally into the site.

Although the site was realised entirely in Flash, it supports deep-linking, mouse-wheel and full-screen support as well as the back-button function of the browser. A number of filtering options make searches an easy and convenient experience.

Client
recom GmbH

Credits
Jung von Matt/Neckar
www.jvm-neckar.de
Jens Franke
www.jensfranke.com
Lime |Flavour
www.limeflavour.com

Awards
FWA, New York Festivals

www.recom.de

977

Percent increase
in site visits

330

Percent increase in
pages viewed per visit

7:16

Minutes average
time on site

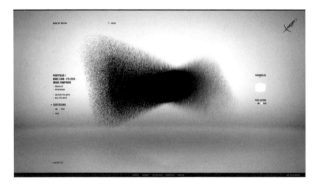

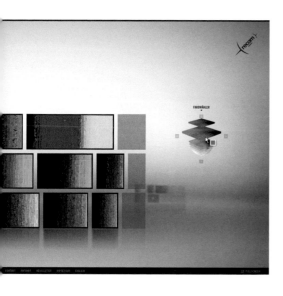

The Solution
The new CMS-based full-Flash page connects the three units recom POST, recom CGI, and recom ART. Intelligent features make it a highly functional tool for recom's customers. The new website concept also has a "pixel mode" in which photos are formed pixel by pixel, picking up the thought of "precision to the very last detail" that is part of recom's mission statement. The site also incorporates familiar search criteria and elements (e.g. the search by photographer, or a lightbox) as well as detailed information about the projects and the company. In addition, new features like the "colour cube" allow users to search the recom archive by colours.

The Results
Although recom did not advertise the new website (aside from the regular newsletter to customers), the number of visitors almost instantly went through the ceiling. Figures usually known only from former Eastern Bloc elections made clear that the relaunch of the website had been long overdue and that clients were eager to try out and use the new site.

Customer comments showed that the all-new recom.de offered them an entirely new level of information about recom's exceptional body of work and gave them new insights into the numerous technical and professional services they offer.

Philips, A Simple Switch

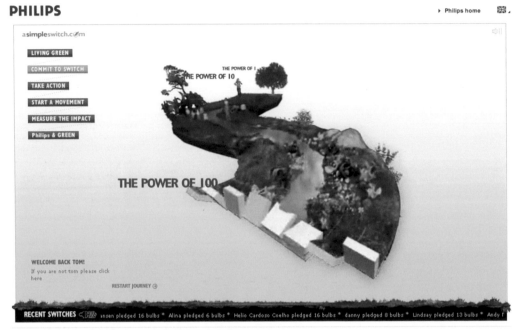

"We believe that big changes start small and that every one of us should contribute to saving our planet."
Gerard Kleisterlee, CEO Philips

The Brief

Environmental issues like global warming are hot topics amongst consumers and have become a discriminator in the battle for brand preference. Main competitors had started to show their "green face" to the consumer. Unlike many other companies, Philips has a long and tangible track record on sustainability. Today the company has more than 200 top-line green products on the market.

So how to promote energy-saving lighting products and emphasise the commitment and efforts of Philips Lighting as a company that genuinely cares about sustainability and energy efficiency? By combining consumer insights with Philips' heritage in sustainability and their green portfolio of lighting products into a practical solution that embraces the brand promise of "sense and simplicity".

The Challenge

Environmentally friendly behaviour on a personal level is complex, diffuse, and confusing: where do I start? What can I do? And what is my impact? Whilst coping, consumers carry the feeling that some solutions are imperfect and the results are not always as expected. These nagging frustrations can leave them with the feeling that the effort is not worthwhile and ultimately lead to a sense of loss of control.

The challenge was to stimulate people and industry all over the world to change their mindset and energy behaviour. Philips Lighting set out to approach the topic of energy efficiency in a simple, unconventional manner. Rather than talk about green issues, the company wanted to make a real difference by showing simplicity matters.

Client
Philips

Credits
Tribal DDB Worldwide
www.tribalddb.com
unit9
www.unit9.com

Awards
FWA, Campaign Digital,
Creative Review, One Show,
Cannes, Design Week, LIA

http://make.asimpleswitch.com

05 Corporate

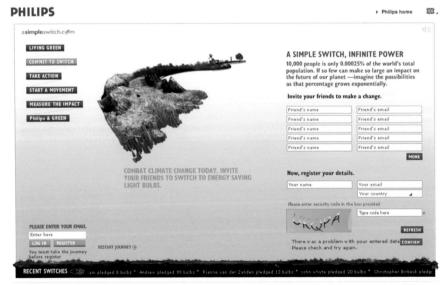

910,000 — Site visits

850,000 — Pledges made

3.3 Million light bulb switches

20 Percent increase in green product sales

The Solution

We created a global movement. The website offers simple steps to a more sustainable lifestyle and motivates visitors to invite friends to do the same. Visitors can "commit to switch" any number of bulbs on the site and see a dramatic demonstration of how their switches impact on both the local and the global environment. The site also tracks how many switches a person's social network has contributed, how many bulbs their friends have pledged to switch, how many bulbs their friends' friends have switched, and so on. Eventually a global map visualises the impact a person and his/her social network can have on our environment for doing something as simple as... switching a light bulb.

The Results

The campaign kicked off in May 2007 with a press conference in New York and an internal employee notification to proudly announce the Live Earth Sponsorship. Philips is founding partner and financial supporter of this initiative with outstanding environmental credentials. This resulted in 2 million audience members and 2 billion viewers, and over 535 million impressions during the main campaign period (July-November). A 20% increase in green product sales. 60% of the visitors indicate they would revisit the website in the coming weeks and almost three out of five will most probably tell relatives and friends about "A Simple Switch". Two out of five also indicate they would invite relatives to join their movement via the website.

05 Corporate

AT&T – Your digital world

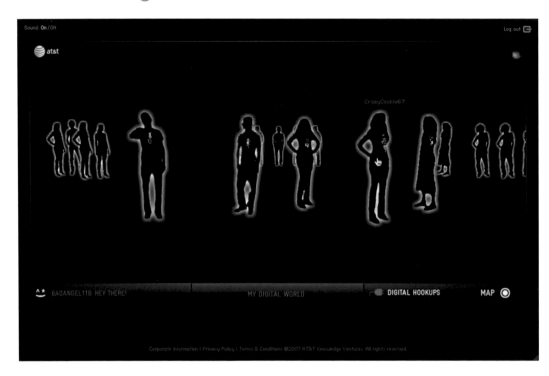

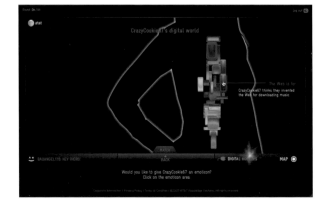

Client
AT&T

Credits
Atmosphere BBDO
www.atmospherebbdo.com
BBDO New York
www.bbdo.com
unit9
www.unit9.com

www.unit9.com/archives/att

> "The new initiatives are designed to highlight how AT&T helps connect people to their worlds wherever they live and work."
> Randall Stephenson,
> AT&T Chairman and CEO

The Brief

Teens are becoming important independent decision makers. Our youth have grown up around technology and cell phones and make heavy use of enhanced features such as IM, the Internet, images and video, ringtones, answer-tones. It's all about staying current, cool, and establishing their social network. Their lives revolve around staying connected to their friends, their music, their style, their family, their unique world.

The AT&T brand is perceived as more their parents' brand than theirs. AT&T wants to shift teen perceptions by introducing their brand and brand benefits as a more relevant and essential part of every youth's world.

The Challenge

Since the re-absorption of the youth-focused Cingular brand, AT&T has been working to contemporize its image among younger consumers. There are many challenges: the audience is savvy and cynical and not a fan of the brand, they don't see it as young and contemporary or cool. So the campaign needs in the first instance to push beyond the barrier of preconceptions even to allow for engagement. Once this has been achieved, the bigger challenge remains to create an online experience that appeals to Web-savvy college audiences and finds a useful way of leveraging existing social networks, not competing with them.

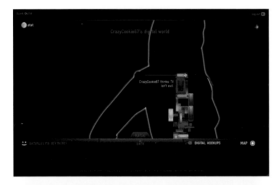

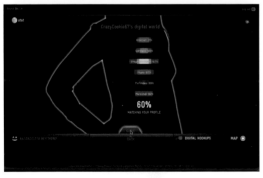

AT&T – Your digital world

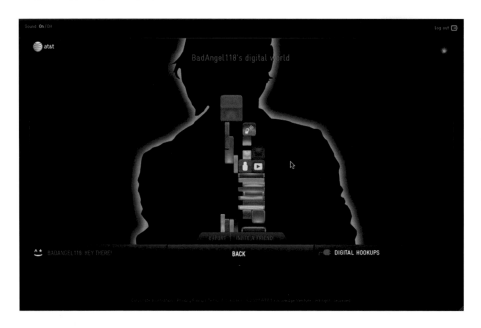

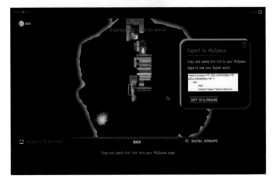

The Solution

The print and outdoor campaign driving traffic to the website did not include a logo, simply a silhouette and the URL address. AT&T as a facilitator, your digital world is an online tool that helps you express your unique digital personality.

Create online personas that visualize how you use the digital world. Whether you're texting, hanging out with friends, or surfing the Web, build your personalized digital strand today to show everyone what you're really like.

Each digital world is created based on a series of questions the user answers about themselves, like gaming, music, and staying in touch with friends. They can then export the color module as an unbranded rich media banner to embed in their favorite social networking platform for others to see.

The Results

The AT&T "Your Digital World" online campaign had a successful branding impact on the young target (13-24); this audience displayed significant increases in all awareness metrics and most brand perceptions, which ultimately drove Brand Favorability. Exposure to the Digital World microsite led to a significant increase in Recommendation Intent. Those who opt in receive incentives and details about AT&T products and services that match their interests, such as special offers on text messages.

Exposure to the campaign was particularly effective among 13-15-year-old males. Slightly over half of visitors to the site agreed the site experience was "interesting" and "memorable" and stated that the website gave them "a positive impression of the sponsor's brand". 10,000 active users and 500 banners exported to MySpace generated an incredibly high number of free Impressions: 1,298,938.

970,719 Site visits

10,000 Active users

5 Percent of users exporting banners

1.3 Million impressions from exported banners

15 Average questions answered

Hyundai Genesis

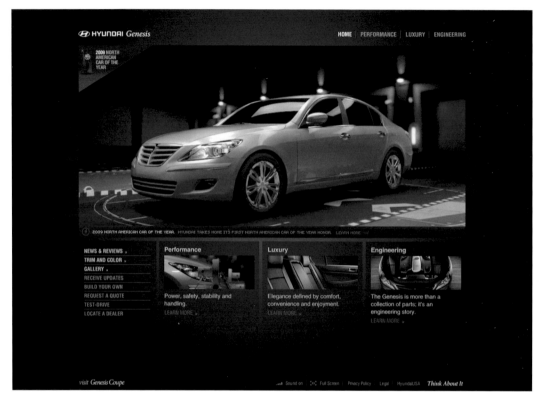

"The Genesis site took a great car and made it a great car that everyone was talking about."
Chris Perry, Dir. Marketing Communications, Hyundai Motor America

The Brief

Hyundai is launching the Genesis, a category-shocking, party-crashing 375-horsepower luxury-performance sedan that is evidence of Hyundai's thoughtful approach to making cars. As Jonathan Swift said, "He was a brave man who first ate an oyster!" – the first to purchase a Genesis will be similarly brave. Going against popular convention to purchase "such an expensive Hyundai", these early adopters will some day be viewed as smart for spending $35–40K for something that competes with cars costing far more. We need to use our interactive work to surprise these consumers, pique their interest, and get them talking about this car. Ultimately, we want them to dive in for a closer look.

The Challenge

When Hyundai told us they were introducing a luxury car, we couldn't help but be a little bit skeptical. And they were our client; what would an everyday person think? So we set out to dispel any and all doubts about the new Hyundai Genesis… including our own. Hyundai is known for making reliable, affordable cars, but the name doesn't exactly inspire images of Rivieras and caviar. True luxury was completely new territory. This was one of the biggest launches in the history of the company. It could either elevate the entire brand, or flop like a flat tire. But how do you convince people that a great luxury car can come from Hyundai?

Client
Hyundai

Credits
Goodby, Silverstein & Partners
www.goodbysilverstein.com
GrupoW
www.grupow.com
Reality Digital
www.realitydigital.com

Awards
FWA, Creative Review Annual

http://hyundaigenesis.com/sedan

The Solution

To convince people to get into the Genesis, we turned to an old and often forgotten tool of persuasion: facts.

We began by dismantling the entire Genesis, piece by piece, and capturing it on film. Users could then zoom in and take a closer look at almost every part. Next, we turned to the experts, filming them as they talked about the Genesis and drove it around.

Then we let people test the car themselves by placing the Genesis on a sadistic interactive treadmill, mimicking the real physics of the car as users took the Genesis around turns and over bumps.

Finally, we placed users inside the car where the horn could be honked, windows rolled down, and the radio turned on, just as if they were really there.

The Results

At the end of this process, we'd managed to convince ourselves that Hyundai had built a pretty great car. And it seems we convinced a few others too.

Who are we to say our site had anything to do with it, but the Hyundai Genesis was named the 2008 North American Car of the Year. A pretty big turnaround when compared to the lukewarm press it received prior to the launch.

And in spite of a downturn across the industry, Hyundai sales went up. In fact, in September, Hyundai actually had higher sales in 2008 than they did in 2007. How many companies can say that?

9 Percent increase in purchase decision

2 Million unique site visits

4:38 Minutes time on site

EA Mobile

"Fi transformed what was essentially a flat catalog site into a true mobile entertainment portal."
Ian Larson, Producer

The Brief

Electronic Arts, one of the biggest gaming distributors, teamed up with Fi to redesign EA Mobile's portal. EA required a consistent cross-platform experience, seamlessly accessible from Web to mobile. In addition to featuring the latest information about games and tips, the new EA Mobile had to allow users to sort and purchase games based on their specific handheld device.

The Challenge

EA Mobile creates and sells around 150 different titles across many dozens of different devices for 12 different carriers. Creating a lightweight, e-commerce-focused cross-platform is a standard challenge in the increasing age of omnipresent digital presence. The greater challenge for this project was that our particular demographic spanned the gamut, featuring an impulsive, fickle audience of casual gamers requiring intuitive shortcuts to purchase. Realizing a visitor would be quickly fed up with the site if they couldn't locate the exact game for their particular device, we realized findability was to be our greatest focus.

Client
Electronic Arts

Credits
Fi
www.f-i.com

www.eamobile.com/Web/
mobile-games

The Solution

In creating a cross-platform experience, we decided on using a compressed JavaScript coupled with light graphics to ensure the site was speedy and consistent. A combination of Actionscript, Flash, Ajax, and XHTML/CSS, Fi's solution was a focused sales-driven experienced skin to entice and appeal to newcomers and casual gamers alike. Fi took a very complicated set of SKUs and presented them to the user in a clean, simple, effective way. Users can simply enter their phone number and the site will do most of the work for them. Users can also enter their phone number, and the site will automatically filter the games available for their specific mobile device.

The Results

Post launch, the site's traffic has increased by 180%, resulting in a critical boost in e-commerce sales. The site set the foundation for a successful collaboration between Electronic Arts and Fi, resulting in multiple future engagements, including EA.com and Spore Origins.

180 — Percent traffic increase

50 — Percent users from USA

2 — Million Google results

NHS EventManager

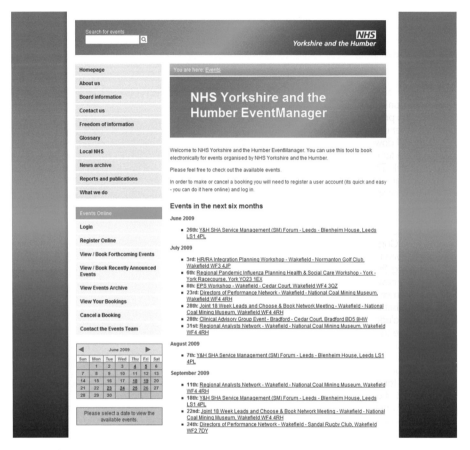

"EventManager is used widely in SHAs and a number of NHS organisations across England. We think it's a great system as it removes the administration burden attached with events and workshops, especially when you are organising a number of large conferences, workshops or training sessions."
Lindsey Atkins, NHS East of England

Client
National Health Service
(NHS), England

Credits
Kent House
www.kenthouse.com

Awards
Medilink West Midlands Award for
NHS Breakthrough, 2008

www.kenthouse.com/event-manager

The Brief

In 2003 a number of NHS organisations consulted Kent House about their difficulty with setting up, organising, and managing high-profile NHS events. NHS staff were spending many hours manually inputting bookings into spreadsheets or databases and then emailing people to confirm that their places had been booked. This process was very time consuming and rather unsystematic. Event managers were bogged down with routine tasks, leaving little time for more strategic and value-added work. The NHS organisations wanted a software system that would be tailored to their needs, hosted and managed for them via the software-as-a-service model, upgraded on a regular basis and supported by an external team of experienced event managers. Consequently, Kent House started working with the NHS Primary Care Contracting Team on the list of requirements for the new event management system. After numerous days of collaboration, it was decided that the event management system would include such fundamental features as: online sign-up, account management, and self-booking for users; controlled access to administration facilities, with different levels for different users; management of quotas for events and accommodation; management of documents related to an event; tracking of attendance/cancellation/no-shows; automated production of delegates lists, catering requirements, special needs; and online generation and reporting of feedback from attendees.

The Challenge

The biggest challenge in developing a tailor-made event management system was a constantly growing list of requirements. As both Kent House and the client were testing the functionality of the newly-delivered event management system, a plethora of new "must-have" and "nice-to-have" features started to emerge. For example, one of the initial requirements for the software was that event delegates would receive email confirmation of their bookings and the receipt of any changes done to their online account. However, shortly after testing this feature, it was decided that the system should also have the capacity to issue short SMS messages to inform delegates about any changes to their booking information or to the event in general. It could be said that the development of the event management system was a great learning process for both parties and certainly one that required a constant re-writing of the system's specification.

9,000 — Events handled

2 — Million bookings

9 — Large NHS organisation users

1.8 — Million registrations

2 — Million pounds saved to date

The Solution

In line with the clients' requirements, Kent House devised a Web-based event management system, EventManager, which can be used to set up, organise, and manage events. The system is very usable and it "understands" the needs and ways of working of event managers as it has been designed and continues to be designed and influenced by event managers for event managers. Using EventManager is easy, and it is accessible from anywhere in the world on any computer with an Internet connection. In addition to providing software that manages events, Kent House offers its clients access to the company's experienced, in-house event managers who are on call to give professional advice and assistance for the duration of events.

The Results

EventManager is now being used to manage much of the NHS' national and regional programmes for training, communicating, and sharing. Although EventManager was initially developed for the NHS Primary Care Contracting Team, it is currently running for eight more NHS organisations, including: NHS Connecting for Health, Strategic Health Authorities, and The National Patient Safety Agency. It is also used by a couple of healthcare-related commercial organisations. The system uses online delivery, automation, collaboration, and self-service to enable cost-effective operation of large programmes of events. The software-as-a-service model behind EventManager allows for efficient maintenance, support, and continuous updating. Success in the NHS is evidenced by it selling on recommendation and having become the norm for delivery of NHS events. In the six years from its first launch, EventManager has handled over two million bookings and 9,000 events and it is cheaper per booking than any of the online alternatives available for busy events teams. It can easily help organisations save net £200,000 per annum.

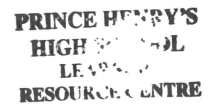

Afterword

by <u>Lars Bastholm</u>, Ogilvy

Afterword

The challenging thing about books like this is how fast they go from being a primer on the state-of-the-art to a history book. If you are reading this in 2010, you might find inspiration for your next project. However, if you're reading it in 2020, it probably seems a little quaint. And that's how it must be.

I recently found The Internet Yellow Pages from 1996, while doing a little house cleaning. It tried to capture every single website out there and categorize it for an easy overview of this new-fangled Internet thing. As absurd as it seems today, surely someone thought back then that it was a great new business idea. On the other hand, I also found a book called Marketing on the Internet from 1997. Flicking through it, I began reading the chapter on "Communities" and quickly realized that it was effectively describing what we're now calling "social media". Terminology and technology might change rapidly, but basic human needs and desires, such as the urge to congregate and talk to like-minded other people, tends to stay the same.

> **"Terminology and technology might change rapidly, but basic human needs and desires, such as the urge to congregate and talk to like-minded other people, tends to stay the same."**

So if nothing else, this book serves as a great documentation of where we are right now (2009). In a medium as transient as the Internet, having books like this is what helps us remember where we came from. Which is often how we find out where we're going.

Most people think it's much younger, but this year marks the 40th anniversary of the Internet. Well, not the Internet as we know it today. That didn't happen till Tim Berners-Lee invented the World Wide Web in the early '90s. But 40 years ago, DARPA successfully sent "packets" of information between two computers, kick-starting what has been the most revolutionary technological invention since electricity. The Internet has literally changed everything, and few aspects of human life have not somehow been impacted or irrevocably altered by it.

Sometimes I feel sorry for everyone working in digital advertising/marketing. Rarely, if ever, has any industry had to re-learn their trade as often as we have over the last 15 years or so. From the simple HTML sites that we used to do in the mid-nineties to some of the insanely technically and conceptually complicated brand experiences showcased in this book, it's been a journey of discovery for everyone, and our toolbox has been expanding unbelievably quickly.

A few years ago, we were still looking at postage stamp-sized videos that took forever to load (remember the World Wide Wait?) and most corporate websites were little more than brochure-ware stitched together with whatever budget and materials were left over from the above-the-line campaign. It took years of relentless innovation, tenacity, salesmanship and, most importantly, changing consumer habits and demands to get us to where we are today.

"The Internet has literally changed everything, and few aspects of human life have not somehow been impacted or irrevocably altered."

I think we have now arrived at a moment of reckoning of sorts. We've reached the kind of technological maturity that effectively means that if we can dream it, we can create it. This is obviously a wonderful thing, but it's also a challenge for all of us. While we were held back by technological limitations, even small dreams looked like big achievements when they were brought to life. Now, we have no more excuses. We need to dream big dreams.

For that we need big dreamers. We need more Tim Berners-Lees, more Sergei Brins and Larry Pages. But we also need our own Bill Bernbach, our own David Ogilvy, and our own Lee Clow. Not to mention our own James Cameron, Steven Spielberg, and Quentin Tarantino. People who dream big in technology, communication, and storytelling and who can help define what this medium will become in the future.

Let's keep in mind that the Internet as a brand-building medium is still only about 15 years old. It remains an unruly teenager trying to figure out its place in the world and what it all means. It's trying out being different things: a TV channel, a community center, a shopping mall, and anything else that might tickle its fancy for a while. So everything is possible, and the wonderful news is that we've only just scratched the surface of the medium's potential.

> "**Every year, without fail, someone asks me for predictions about what will happen online in the next 12 months. And every year, I refuse to take the bait.**"

Every year, without fail, someone asks me for predictions about what will happen online in the next 12 months. And every year I refuse to take the bait. You see, it's hard to make predictions, especially about the future (a line I've appropriated from Danish writer Storm P). If I get it wrong, I lose. If I get it right, they'll come back year after year, until I get it wrong. Either way I lose eventually, so why even try?

There will always be dreamers sitting in a garage, cooking up something that will trigger a paradigm shift for how we work, and what we produce. No one saw YouTube coming. No one saw Google becoming the biggest player in online advertising. No one expected Twitter to become a global phenomenon. That's just the way it works in this industry.

So here's to the dreamers, to the ones that come up with a simple idea that changes the way people interact. To the ones who decide that everything we know is wrong and zig instead of zagging. To the ones who want to tell stories in new and unexplored ways.

I can't wait to see what you'll come up with next.

Lars Bastholm
Ogilvy

Bio.
Lars Bastholm
Chief Digital Creative Officer,
Ogilvy North America

In 2009 Lars Bastholm joined Ogilvy North America in a specially created role as Chief Digital Creative Officer with responsibility for Ogilvy's digital creative work across North America.

Lars has been working in the interactive marketing industry for over 13 years. After starting up Grey Interactive in Scandinavia, he joined Framfab in Copenhagen, Denmark, as Creative Director. There he worked on some of the world's most recognized brands, including Nike, LEGO, Coca-Cola, and Carlsberg.

Lars is one of the most award-winning creatives in the digital marketing industry, with a multitude of international awards to his name, including no less than three Cyber Lions Grands Prix from Cannes.

In 2004 Lars was hired to open up an AKQA office in New York. He grew the office successfully, pitching and winning global AOR relationships with clients like Coca-Cola, Smirnoff, and Motorola. Lars left AKQA as the Co-Chief Creative Officer in March 2009.

Lars has judged all the major international award shows, and he is a frequent speaker at industry events. Lars most recently joined the Ad Council's Campaign Review Committee to ensure the integrity and creativity of the Ad Council's public service advertising.
–
www.ogilvy.com

"We have no more excuses. We need to dream big dreams."

Creating a second book is always harder than putting the first together, especially when the first one was such a tremendous success. This has been the case with this book, the follow-up to *Guidelines for Online Success* that received so many good reviews and already registers over 14,000 results on a Google search.

We still remember sipping tea and eating cakes in Cambridge when we sketched out the concept for this second volume, just a few months after the release of *Guidelines for Online Success*. The main idea was still about enabling this complicated dialogue between clients, designers, and anyone interested in the Web. But this time, instead of guidelines, we would feature some insider stories, from briefing to results, going through the challenges and the solutions every project battles with. We felt it was also crucial to have numbers/statistics attached to every case study, so that they would be measurable for readers. Moreover, we made sure that we had a large range and diversity of sites, both in size (smaller as well as giant projects) and in fields (from corporate to social media, via e-commerce, campaigns, and promotional sites).

We need to thank a lot of people, without whom this book wouldn't have been possible. First of all we would like to thank all the contributors for their dedication and attention to the importance of the publication: you have all made this publication a groundbreaking one. We would also like to thank specifically Chris Allen (for his proof-reading eagle eye on the manuscript), Jutta Hendricks (for her impeccable work with the texts), Olivier Marchand and Benjamin Laugel (from Soleil Noir, for the final review of the French version), Hugo Olivera (for the final review of the Spanish version), Kai Heuser (for the final review of the German version), Jürgen Dubau (for the German translation), Equipo de Edición (for the French and Spanish translations), Stefan Klatte (our man on the production front), and Jon Cefai at KentLyons (for once again designing an amazing-looking book).

A *very* special thanks goes to Daniel Siciliano Bretas, our right-hand at all times and the manager of the whole book. Without him the book would not have got off the ground in the first place. His work and great attention to detail makes this book a special one.

Rob Ford & Julius Wiedemann

© 2010 TASCHEN GmbH
Hohenzollernring 53
D-50672 Köln
www.taschen.com

Design by KentLyons

Editor
Rob Ford
Julius Wiedemann
Editorial Coordination
Daniel Siciliano Bretas
Collaboration
Jutta Hendricks
English Proof-reader
Chris Allen
Production
Stefan Klatte

Printed in China
ISBN 978-3-8365-1895-6

To stay informed about
upcoming TASCHEN titles,
please request our magazine
at www.taschen.com/magazine
or write to TASCHEN America,
6671 Sunset Boulevard, Suite
1508, USA-Los Angeles, CA
90028, contact-us@taschen.
com, Fax: +1-323-463.4442.
We will be happy to send you
a free copy of our magazine
which is filled with information
about all of our books.